How to
be a Walking
Advertisement
for Jesus

ACT NOW!

Offer Ends Soon!

GINGER SINSABAUGH

Regal

A Division of Gospel Light
Ventura, California, U.S.A.

PUBLISHED BY REGAL BOOKS
A DIVISION OF GOSPEL LIGHT
VENTURA, CALIFORNIA, U.S.A.
PRINTED IN U.S.A.

Regal Books is a ministry of Gospel Light, an evangelical Christian publisher dedicated to serving the local church. We believe God's vision for Gospel Light is to provide church leaders with biblical, user-friendly materials that will help them evangelize, disciple and minister to children, youth and families.

It is our prayer that this Regal book will help you discover biblical truth for your own life and help you meet the needs of others. May God richly bless you.

For a free catalog of resources from Regal Books and Gospel Light please call your Christian supplier, or contact us at 1-800-4-GOSPEL.

Cover Design by Kevin Keller
Interior Design by Robert Williams
Illustrations by Dan Foote
Edited by David Webb

LIBRARY OF CONGRESS CATALOGING-IN-PUBLICATION DATA
Sinsabaugh, Ginger, 1961–
    Act now! offer ends soon / Ginger Sinsabaugh.
        p.   cm.
    ISBN 0-8307-2427-3 (trade paper)
    1. Witness bearing (Christianity)   I. Title.
    BV4520.S475   1999   99-41512
    269'.2—dc21   CIP

1 2 3 4 5 6 7 8 9 10 11 12 13 14 15 / 05 06 03 02 01 00 99

Rights for publishing this book in other languages are contracted by Gospel Literature International (GLINT). GLINT also provides technical help for the adaptation, translation and publishing of Bible study resources and books in scores of languages worldwide. For further information, write to GLINT at P.O. Box 4060, Ontario, CA 91761-1003, U.S.A. You may also send E-mail to Glintint@aol.com, or visit their website at www.glint.org.

In memory of my Dad

Contents

PART III
FREE INSPIRATIONAL STUFF!

BONUS CHAPTER!

ACKNOWLEDGMENTS

This book was made possible in part by all of my favorite fast foods, all-purpose cleansers, artificial flavors and cream-filled centers. Special thanks go to the World's Greatest Mom, Jeff the Chair Guy and to my editor, David Webb.

Confessions from Madison Avenue

OK. I admit it. I'm in advertising. I am personally responsible for those annoying commercials you see on TV. I've written witty lines for Michael Jordan. I've plugged everything from yogurt to snack foods, from all-purpose cleaners to panty hose. I've made jalapeño peppers dance and cereal elves sing.

I am also a Christian.

Being a Christian, I have a message I want to share that's more important than "Snap! Crackle! Pop!"

That message is the gospel of Jesus Christ.

Sometimes getting people to listen to the gospel seems next to impossible! They think Christianity is boring or not for them. And they are tired of being told they *need* religion like they *need* fiber. Or, worst of all, the basic message of God's love just doesn't grab their attention.

So I started thinking, *If I can get America to listen to a talking cereal, I should be able to get them to listen to me talk about Christ.* For starters, Christianity is far more exciting than any part of a complete breakfast. God can do more for you than eight essential vitamins and iron.

So why not use the tools of advertising to tune people into Christianity? After all, they're nothing but basic rules of communication.

Who knows, if we treated our testimonies the way advertisers do a Big Mac, maybe people would pile into church pews the way they flock to fast-food drive-thrus.

Well, that's what this book is about.

By learning from the things we buy and see on TV, we can make our testimonies as impactful as our favorite commercials. Our message can be as memorable as "Where's the beef?" We don't need megaphones on street corners to get people to listen; all we need is the irresistibility of chocolate cake.

The best part is, we'll be offering people the key to *everlasting* life! Jesus offers savings no coupon can.

So move over Snap, Crackle and Pop.

You're about to learn a few pointers on how to effectively communicate Christ—plus a lot of other fun stuff, too.

And all it's going to take is 30 seconds.

PART I

SEVEN RULES OF ADVERTISING YOUR FAITH

Create a Craving

O taste and see that the LORD is good!
PSALM 34:8

Stop for a minute and think of the commercials you love—the entertaining ones that get you to stop channel surfing for 30 seconds and give the batteries in your remote a well-deserved break. You know, the commercials that make you buy the things you do. Does your favorite ad feature a super athlete or a super-sized burger? Does it tell you about a new flavor of barbeque chips or a new cure for barbeque breath? My personal favorite is the one with that little doughboy who doesn't seem to mind that he's pudgy, let alone naked. He runs around giggling until the cinnamon rolls are ready, but instead of eating them, he's happy just getting poked in the belly! Go figure.

Whether your favorite commercial stars a toucan who sniffs cereal or a snuggly bear who sniffs laundry, the effective ones have the same thing in common: They never force their message on you. They never tell you that you *need* anything; they simply make you *want* it.

I can honestly say that Little Debbie has never had to twist my arm to get me to eat a Nutty Bar. Nor has anyone ever force-fed me a Twinkie. All it takes is one mouth-watering glance at that cream-filled center. Or a quick glimpse of caramel nougat. Just show me a tight shot of a food dehydrator overflowing with beef jerky, and before you know it, you'll have to peel me off the screen.

MMM-MMM GOOD!

For He has satisfied the thirsty soul, and the hungry soul
He has filled with what is good.
PSALM 107:9

Twinkies, Nutty Bars and beef jerky can be quite tasty. But did you know that the Word of God can be just as tempting? The psalmists wrote, "O taste and see that the LORD is good!" (Psalm 34:8) and "How sweet are Your words to my taste!" (Psalm 119:103, *NKJV*). Yet when we tell people about Christ, we often forget those verses and head straight for the passages about guilt,

Just like a cream-filled Twinkie, the Bible is filled with reasons why you should want it. But far too often we get stuck on telling people why they need it.

the wrath of God or eternal damnation. That's like telling a kid he should eat his meatloaf because there are starving kids in China—it doesn't work. Does anyone buy Lucky Charms for the eight important vitamins? No! They're after those tasty marshmallow stars. Sure, I can try to tell people why Lucky Charms is good for them, but there are better things to focus on.

By calling attention to the goodness of God, you'll find it's easier to give your friends reasons why they should want Christ. It's not that Jesus is boring and sticky buns are not. Actually, nothing is more exciting than living for Christ! But telling people they *need* Christ—or anything else, for that matter—is a sure way to turn them off. One of the first things I learned as a copywriter is that if you have to say it's fun, it isn't. If you say it's cool, they'll know it's dorky. If you tell someone they need it, they won't want it. The product ends up sounding dull, like cod-liver oil in a world of colas.

Take my personal relationship with lima beans. I can't stand them because they were something I was forced to eat as a child. A truly tasteless form of torture. My dad would make me sit at the table for hours until they were all gone—and the only thing worse than eating lima beans is eating cold lima beans.

My lingering feelings toward lima beans are not worth going to therapy over; I already know I hate them because they were forced upon me. But I also know that if lima beans had been a treat offered to me as a reward for cleaning my plate, I might be open to eating them today.

HEY, MIKEY! HE LIKES IT!

Remember the classic commercial for Life cereal? Two brothers are pushing a bowl of cereal back and forth because they had heard "It's supposed to be good for you." Neither of them wants to try it, so they give it to their little brother, Mikey, who doesn't know it's good for him. And they find out he likes it—he really likes it!

Well, Life cereal and the Book of life have a lot in common. If you want people to try it, don't make them think they need it. Make them want to dig in for themselves.

FREE WILLS AND FREE SNACKS

Ever wonder why there are so many varieties of fruit-flavored snacks? Fuzz-free peach taffy, wobbly watermelon chews, banana-tangerine frozen juice bars . . . and what's with those orange Circus Peanuts? Let's just say advertisers make the most of your free will.

God created free will. He gave it to Adam; He gave it to Eve. They were free to choose whatever fruit snack they desired. Unfortunately, they made the worst possible choice. And yet God didn't rescind His offer of free will; we still have a choice. That's why it's important that the gospel message be more desirable than an apple (or a quince).

Think about it for a moment. What was it about the Christian life that first got your attention? What was it that appealed to you?

WHY I CRAVED THE CHRISTIAN LIFE

When I think of the person in my life who played the biggest part in leading me to Christ, I chuckle. As I was growing up, I paid little attention to the people who told me I needed Jesus, but when I was in college, I finally listened to one young woman who simply made me want what I lacked. You can charge me with breaking the tenth commandment, but I coveted her happiness.

Now, I'm sure you've heard my brand of testimony before: I grew up in a typical Christian family. Went to church. Memorized verses. Even saw *A Thief in the Night* three times. Christianity was something everyone said I needed. My parents said I needed it. My friends said I needed it. Billy Graham said I needed it. The guy on the street corner with a megaphone said I needed it. But it was never something I really *wanted*. Before long, church became a place where I sat listlessly until Mom's Sunday roast was done, and Christianity became nothing more than another belief system with a few major holidays.

So, I went to college, putting my relationship with God on the back burner in an age of microwave ovens. During my senior year at Michigan State University, only weeks before I was to graduate, I found myself in trouble and was about to be thrown off campus. I had hosted a party in the dormitory that I, uh, really shouldn't have. Everyone short of the dorm director was there. Alcohol was flowing and the party was in full swing—until the dorm director showed up. As I faced suspension, I feared the worst.

But someone stepped in and went to bat for me: an optimistic young lady who was nothing at all like me. She didn't drink, didn't smoke, didn't swear, didn't consume any of the things I lived for. She even ate the dorm food without complaining! She was my resident hall assistant and she was a Christian. For the life of me, I can't remember her name, and to this day I doubt whether she knows the effect she had on my life.

As she reviewed with me the university policy regarding parties, as well as the dangers of drinking, not once did she berate or belittle me. There was something genuinely different about her: She always seemed happy without indulging in the vices common to college students. Her happiness was founded in her relationship with Christ and she didn't get in the way of allowing others to see it. There were no tracts slipped under my door; her testimony was in her actions.

She didn't judge me. In fact, she saved my neck, preventing my suspension. As a good witness of Christ, she saved much more.

I didn't know my resident hall assistant well, but I knew that I wanted what she had. Not needed, but wanted. That's when I first craved the Lord—and now I can't get enough! *Yo quiero* Jesus Christ!

SEEKING VS. SEEKING COVER

Let the heart of those who seek the Lord be glad.

PSALM 105:3

Sometimes when we share the gospel message, we become so excited that a living, breathing person actually wants to hear it that we blow our big chance. We can get so carried away listing all the reasons why people need Christ that we never make them want Christ. Our captive audience ends up feeling trapped and instead of seeking Christ, they seek cover.

It's just like the friend that's always selling you Tupperware. How many airtight cucumber keepers do you really need? But you ended up buying another one out of guilt, thinking you'd give it to your mother-in-law for her birthday. Eventually, you stop answering the door when that friend stops by because she's pushing plastic. That's seeking cover. But *seeking* is another story.

Christ was big on the word "seek." "Ask, and it shall be given to you," He said. "Seek, and you shall find; knock, and it shall be opened to you" (Matthew 7:7). Jesus knew the importance of letting us do the seeking. He put us in the driver's seat.

Face it, no one goes out seeking halitosis or embarrassing denture odor. You only seek what looks good and what feels good, whether it's a Whopper or the Word of God. So if a nonbeliever sees what you have in Christ and wants it, too, before long they'll be seeking Him.

THE SECRET INGREDIENT

Granted, there are some things we're better off not knowing, like what kind of animal Spam actually is. Or just what makes Jell-O jiggle. Then there are those secrets that you *do* want to know. For instance, just what are the 57 ingredients in Heinz 57 Steak

Sauce? Sorry, it's a secret recipe. If you call up Heinz (like I did) and ask what's in it, they will kindly say, "We're not telling."

Secret recipes (and secrets in general) are irresistible. As a Christian, you hold the secret to an irresistible way of life—a life people will crave, just the way I craved the lifestyle of the nice young woman whose name I can't remember. If they can see Christ in you and hear Him in your words, they will know there's something different about you. They won't be able to put their finger on exactly what it is, but they'll want it.

This is one secret too good to keep to yourself. Share it with a couple of friends. And make them promise to tell two friends. And *they'll* tell two friends. And so on, and so on . . . .

A FINAL LESSON FROM LITTLE DEBBIE

Ahhh, my favorite indulgence of all time: Little Debbie's Star Crunches, the poor man's 100 Grand bars. No one stops with one Star Crunch; I've been known to eat an entire box, even though it means spending the next three years at the gym. Obviously, the Bible can't compare to Little Debbie's Star Crunches. It's better—there's no treadmill.

So, take a lesson from Little Debbie. Let your friends crave the guilt-free rewards of Christianity—the joy, the happiness and, of course, all that milk and honey. Focus on the good stuff and they'll be eating it up in no time.

So what's the big trick to advertising? Naked people in ice cubes? I don't think so. Simply make people want something instead of telling them they need it. You don't have to be a giggling doughboy to do that.

THE GOTTA-HAVE-IT CHECKLIST

- Who were the Christians in your life that really got through to you?
- Just how did they do it? Did they show you Christ as something you needed, like cod-liver oil, or like the icing on life's cake?
- What makes the Christian life irresistible to you?
- How can someone's free will work in your favor when sharing Christ?

Know Your Audience

I have become all things to all men, that I may by all means save some.
1 CORINTHIANS 9:22

If you only knew what advertisers know about you. Their meticulous research tells them the difference between people who prefer lemon scent over pine scent. They know how often a teenager worries about pimples vs. worrying about his future. They know how often a single man eats at a fast-food restaurant each week— and how many pickles he prefers on his burger. There are even statistics on those who put toilet paper over the roller vs. under.

Why all the consumer research? Is there really a point to all the surveys and questionnaires? You bet! Advertisers know they can't create an effective message until they know their audience, whether they're talking bubble bath or beliefs. Millions of dollars are spent annually on research, from counting how many times a person chews cereal before swallowing (the more, the better) to the preferred color of window cleaner (purple).

And what's the bottom line to all the research? *People are different.*

Advertisers can assume certain things about their audience based on characteristics like age and sex. One generation tries to keep their pants from bagging, while the other thinks it's the latest rage. Most men enjoy watching other men chase a pigskin across artifical turf on a Sunday afternoon; the average woman, not so much. But that's just the beginning. Research reveals lifestyle choices, tastes and preferences that speak volumes about what a particular demographic group wants out of life. What kind of music do you listen to? What's your favorite TV show? How do you like to spend your free time? Are you married? Do you prefer paper or plastic?

There are those who crave life's salsa and those who want the warmth of mashed potatoes. Some like it hot; some like it cold.

MADISON AVENUE OR GETHSEMANE GARDEN?

Consumer research isn't something concocted by the creative minds of Madison Avenue. Christ was a big proponent of knowing your audience. He knew that different people craved different things. What Christ said to a young fisherman was different from what He told the tax collector in a tree. He knew what He said to a compulsive cleaner should be different from what He said to her socializing sister. Same basic message, different approaches.

The person who eats Doritos is not the person who uses Poly Grip.

Since Christ had different kinds of messages for different audiences, we are blessed with a variety pack of verses in the Bible. The Word of God can speak to any situation, satisfy any spiritual hunger. In it you'll find healing words for the broken-hearted, for the sick, for the widowed, for the lonely; truth for those who are slaves to religion, slaves to their jobs, slaves to their sin. Whatever your audience craves, if know your audience first, you'll have little problem knowing what to say.

The LifeSavers Theory goes like this: The less a speaker knows his audience, the more likely it is that those sitting in the back row are eating LifeSavers. I know the theory holds true because I have been both the ill-prepared speaker and the fidgety LifeSavers eater. Sitting through the Sunday morning service was unbearable for my kid sister and me. We would raid our mother's purse for *anything* to eat (although we stayed away from the unwrapped cough drops permanently stuck to the bottom). We would doodle on the bulletins until our pens went dry. Then we would count the squares of tile on the ceiling of the sanctuary—328. The funny thing is, we were adults at the time.

But knowing your audience doesn't just apply when speaking in a formal setting. You can just as easily alienate someone you are witnessing to one-on-one if you don't know what makes them tick.

YOUNG OR OLD?

Face it. Words that will reach the generation of pierced body parts won't go over well with those who wear Grecian Formula. That's why you seldom see Ronald McDonald and the Hamburglar during commercial breaks on Monday Night Football. A big, beefy burger is more likely to entice the big, beefy audience.

Knowing your audience's age and the tastes of that age group is crucial when creating your message. I learned that one time with talking dummies. Ventriloquists and talking dummies helped to make Vacation Bible School a fond childhood memory for me, and they can still be a big hit with younger children today. But sometimes the puppet isn't the only dummy.

A few years ago, I had the opportunity to speak at a London school on the topic of Christianity. The woman who made this possible insisted that we should use puppetry to reach the youth. This woman *loved* puppets! She had big puppets, little puppets, puppets with googly eyes. She even taught us a few hand exercises for "better puppet action." Since this woman lived in London and knew the school, I assumed she knew what she was talking about when she said puppets would be the perfect way to reach our audience.

So we brought the puppets to school and waited in the auditorium for the kids to arrive. As the auditorium started to fill, I was mortified. These were not cute little children at all, but a group of budding adolescents ready for Puberty 101. They did not like our puppets. Not the big ones, not the little ones. Especially not the one with the googly eyes.

So think, what is the age of the person you are trying to reach? How can you target the gospel precisely for him or her? Get to know the likes and dislikes of your audience, from their taste in music to their taste in pizza toppings. You'll be amazed how the little differences add up.

MALE OR FEMALE?

Strength and dignity are her clothing, and she smiles at the future.
PROVERBS 31:25

Strength and dignity may be her clothing, but figuring out what to make for dinner is always her future. That's why almost every meal product is targeted toward that powerful female consumer better known as Mom.

Surprised? Even in our "enlightened" postmodern age, Mom is most likely to be responsible for cooking, shopping and cleaning up the messes of the household, regardless of her increased duties in the workforce. Mom also knows that the three little words her husband utters to her most often are "What's for dinner?"

So when creating commercials targeted toward moms, advertisers follow this 30-second recipe: Start with one ease-of-preparation scene, add one hungry dad scene and top it off with a one-bite-and-a-smile-from-little-Billy-to-assure-Mom-he-won't-feed-it-to-the-dog scene. But you had better plan on showing hearty portions of tender, juicy beef and sizzling sound effects if you want to grab the attention of Mom's male counterpart.

OK, as an advertiser I have at my disposal reams of research that tells me what men want. But as a woman, what do I *really* know about men? Nothing. But I once found myself in an unusual predicament in Bulgaria when I was asked at a moment's notice to speak to several hundred teenage boys about sex. The first thought that ran through my mind was *What's an American woman going to teach Bulgarian boys about sex?* So I turned the tables and used to my advantage the awkwardness of being a woman speaking on the subject of sex to a group of hormonally charged adolescent males.

Not being a young Bulgarian male, I was clueless as to the rituals and rules of the Black Sea dating scene, so I asked them to explain things to me. I used my lack of knowledge to ask them questions about male behavior: What does it feel like to get a girl pregnant and leave her? What is going through a young man's mind when he sweet-talks a girl one night, knowing that he'll brag to his friends about "scoring" the next morning? I asked because I truly didn't know. I was only familiar with the female end of the stick, and that side isn't always pretty.

It worked. The boys and I all learned something by taking advantage of our gender differences. Yes, the gender of an audience does matter when designing your message, especially when you're sharing the gospel. Men will usually be drawn to the courage of Christ, while most women will be taken with His compassion. This sounds obvious, but it's so often overlooked.

A CURRENT CONSUMER OR A NEW CONVERT?

What you will say to someone who believes in a product is different from what you will say to someone who does not, whether it's the Word of God or yogurt.

I have had the strange thrill of sitting behind a two-way mirror many times, listening to women spill their guts about their first experiences eating yogurt. (And you thought the afternoon talk shows got all the good topics.) Many women confessed to having tried yogurt in the mid-1970s when it was widely introduced in America and their memories were not pleasant. Yogurt back then was lumpy, extremely sour and, well, repulsive. In other words, their first taste of yogurt left a bad taste in their mouths. That's why many of these women haven't touched yogurt since. (Of course, in recent years, yogurt has changed. It's smoother, sweeter and comes in more flavors than you can shake a spoon at. If these women only knew what they were missing . . .)

The same holds true with a person's first taste of Christianity. If religion has left a bad taste in the mouth of your audience, getting them to listen will be more difficult than getting the attention of someone who has never experienced church.

Unfortuanately, PKs (pastor's kids) can be easily soured on the church experience. Three siblings grew up in a church where their father was the pastor. Though their dad was incredible behind the pulpit, he showed a different, most unpleasant face at home. These children grew up in an atmosphere of hypocrisy instead of experiencing the sincere love of God. Now that they are teens, they have no desire to try church again. Getting them to open up to the gospel is extremely difficult and finding a new way to serve it up is a constant challenge. But someday these young people will get another taste of the Word of God and see that it is good.

Find out whether your audience has ever gone to church before. Was it a sour experience or was it good? And would they be willing to try it again?

ONE-ON-ONE RESEARCH

Don't make the mistake of assuming everyone is like you. Know your audience, whether it's your best friend, some fellow Bible study members or a pretzel-crunching puppet lover. Knowing who they are will help you get through to them.

AUDIENCE HELPER

Whoever your audience is, there's something in the Bible just for them. Here's a sampler:

- Single Moms: "He supports the fatherless and the widow" (Psalm 146:9).
- Thirty Something and Still Single: "House and wealth are an inheritance from fathers, but a prudent wife is from the LORD" (Proverbs 19:14).

- Bad Hair Day: "Charm is deceitful and beauty is vain, but a woman who fears the LORD, she shall be praised" (Proverbs 31:30).
- Bad Day in General: "[Cast] all your anxiety upon Him, because He cares for you" (1 Peter 5:7).
- Teenagers: "Let no one look down on your youthfulness, but rather in speech, conduct, love, faith and purity, show yourself an example of those who believe" (1 Timothy 4:12).
- Parents of a Teenager: "And if he sins against you seven times a day, and returns to you seven times, saying, 'I repent,' forgive him" (Luke 17:4).
- I've Fallen and I Can't Get Up: "For all have sinned and fall short of the glory of God" (Romans 3:23).

Chapter 3

Keep It Simple

For God is not a God of confusion but of peace.
1 CORINTHIANS 14:13

In this complex world, the idea that a product can in some way simplify our lives is enough to get most people to try just about anything. That's exactly what enticed me to buy a Simplicity dress pattern. As a beginning sewer, I was blessed with more enthusiasm than experience. I assumed the name Simplicity meant it was an idiot-proof pattern. Boy, was I wrong! Before I knew it, I was up to my elbows in paisley. I couldn't make sense of the pieces or the pattern, let alone tell you where to pin a puffed-sleeve hole. So, I threw everything into a box and shipped it to Simplicity headquarters with a short but pointed letter. It read: "Dear Simplicity, if you are so simplistic, *you* sew it or change your name to Catastrophe."

Simple sells. It brings order to our chaos, makes sense out of nonsense and transforms the overwhelming, boiling it down to one easily digestible point. It's the difference between a grandé mocha cappuccino latte and a cup of coffee. It's the reason why you can remember the Slinky song but have no idea where you just put your car keys.

Simple can also mean the difference between a seeker hearing the gospel or not.

SLICING AND DICING A MESSAGE

Not all television commercials stick to the principle of "simple sells," but those that don't are often the commercials that most annoy us or, worse yet, can't convince us. Like those spots for Japanese steak knives that slice up the message like julienne fries—we find it hard to believe that one set of knives can fillet a wide-mouth bass *and* create roses out of radishes. Nor do we care. Then there are those car commercials that spend so much time explaining finance options that they miss the big message: cars for sale.

It's important to remember this principle of simplicity when sharing your faith with others. Keeping your message simple is crucial to its impact.

GOD KEPT THINGS SIMPLE

Ever wonder why the book of Genesis doesn't dwell on the details of how God hung the stars? Probably because God knew such minutiae would bore teenagers and baffle the shepherds and fishermen who would build His kingdom. Instead, God simplified creation, boiling all the astrophysics and quantum mechanics down to one simple verse:

In the beginning God created the heavens and the earth (Genesis 1:1).

God told us just enough about the process of creation to keep our interest piqued rather than overwhelm us with the principles of self-sustaining ecosystems. I, for one, could not bear to sit through a sermon explaining how and why God made the boll weevil.

God kept the creation story simple and it has remained approachable—and popular—for centuries. You don't need an advanced degree in genetic engineering to understand it. Speculative, theoretical discussions as to whether Adam and Eve had belly buttons (and, if so, why) should be confined to seminaries and creationist think tanks. God didn't let minutiae obscure His message. And if the Almighty didn't explain everything, then maybe you don't have to, either.

THE AUTHORS OF CONFUSION

Our God is a God of love and peace (see 2 Corinthians 13:11), but there are also gods of confusion better known as junior advertising executives. I sat in a meeting where these young, ambitious college grads spent hours arguing passionately over how to sell instant mashed potatoes. One ad exec wanted to emphasize the "newness" of the instant potato flakes. Another insisted we focus on how there were three flavors. Yet another wanted to emphasize the "excitement value" of trying a new product. All were valid points, but when we tried to focus on all three, we transformed our instant potatoes into instant confusion for our audience. We overloaded our 15-second spot with 16 seconds of information, and the chance to grab the audience's attention with our message was missed.

The moral of this tale of advertising woe is this: If you attempt to say too much in too little time, even mashed potatoes can turn into mental mayhem. Let's not make the same mistake when talking about the Sermon on the Mount.

Effective advertising has a single-minded selling proposition—one simple statement, whether it's about the flavor of a potato flake or the springtime freshness of a leading fabric softener. Together, the client, account executives, creative staff and research department must agree on one crucial point to communicate to the audience. They know that by focusing on one simple message, they increase the likelihood of capturing their audience.

CHRIST SIMPLY FOCUSED

Jesus demonstrated how to keep your message simple and focused. He simplified the eternal truths of His kingdom and used everyday language, so that His listeners and future generations of regular guys could grasp His meaning. Take for instance the Beatitudes, nine of the best-known lines from the Sermon on the Mount. Read the following from Matthew 5:3-11, then ask yourself, *Just what part of "blessed" don't I understand?*

Blessed are the poor in spirit, for theirs is the kingdom of heaven.

Blessed are those who mourn, for they shall be comforted.

Blessed are the gentle, for they shall inherit the earth.

Blessed are those who hunger and thirst for righteousness, for they shall be satisfied.

Blessed are the merciful, for they shall receive mercy.

Blessed are the pure in heart, for they shall see God.

Blessed are the peacemakers, for they shall be called sons of God.

Blessed are those who have been persecuted for the sake of righteousness, for theirs is the kingdom of heaven.

Blessed are you when men cast insults at you, and persecute you, and say all kinds of evil against you falsely, on account of Me.

The message is well focused; the wording is basic. Needless to say, Christ's message is easier to remember than the exacting laws set forth in Leviticus.

When you share the gospel message, by simply focusing on one of Christ's timeless attributes, you can leave a bigger impression than if you try to explain the nuances of the apostle Paul's theology. Stick with one simple message to reach your audience. What single saving proposition do you want the hearer to remember?

SIMPLE ENOUGH FOR A CHILD

If you knew everything there is to know about yogurt, you probably would never put it in your mouth. This "cultured" snack treat supplies you with a lot more than just calcium. For example, yogurt is filled with bacteria that does wonderful things for your colon. And it smells like bacteria that does wonderful things for your colon. But instead of telling you everything you never wanted to know about yogurt and never thought to ask, advertisers sort through the nutritional information and benefits to make its appeal simple enough for a child to understand.

Children are a growing market for yogurt. Their growing bodies need the nutrients it supplies and, believe it or not, their tiny taste buds crave the fruity flavors. But if children knew yogurt was full of *bifidus* bacteria as well as blueberries, even more of it would end up on the kitchen floor instead of in their mouths.

We are all precious children in the eyes of the Lord. Sure, there's a lot about God we don't know or fully understand, but there's a lot more that's simple and sweet. So keep your message short and sweet. There's a baby believer out there just waiting to hear it and grow.

AVOID THE FINE PRINT

You see it at the end of car commercials: excruciatingly fine print explaining the terms of 3.9% financing on approved credit and how the offer is void in New Jersey and Alaska. Just who reads that stuff? Probably only the lawyers who made the advertising firm write it in the first place. While such tedious details are important to some, they bore and even alienate the rest of us.

Fine print is equally aggravating to someone interested in hearing the overall message of the Bible. Sometimes, as Christians, we get so enthusiastic about sharing from our gen-

Sharing Christ should be fun—for you and your audience. So take a tip from your bathroom cleanser: Be sure your testimony is quick and powerful, yet nonabrasive.

uine leather, industrial strength, chain reference, New American King James Expanded Living Version Bibles that we miss the big picture: God loves us and sent His Son to save us. Be careful not to overload the nonbeliever with not-so-crucial details. The measurements of Solomon's Temple might interest you, but they won't get your audience to heaven. Neither will a Hebrew word study on the book of Haggai.

True, we don't want people to think that Christmas is a holiday when Jesus comes out and if He sees His shadow, we've got three more months till spring; but we don't want them to think of Christianity as an endless list of restrictive rules and regulations, either. So put the deeper topics on layaway until your audience is ready for them. Until then, focus on how Christ came into the world to save men, not to confuse them.

MISSING THE BIG PICTURE

When you get caught up with details, you can miss the big picture altogether, even when focusing on a single message. This happened to me while working on a cereal that, fortunately, now exists only in the sense memory of a few taste buds. This now-defunct cereal was a mixture of crispy rice and marshmallow fruit shapes. The single selling proposition was simple: lots of fruit taste. To communicate this to kids, our target market, we created a fun commercial featuring a rhumba line of dancing fruit moving to the beat of bongo drums and singing about the taste of the marshmallow shapes.

Well, we sort of got carried away working on the music, which was filled with as many drums as there were opinions on the music. Some in the agency thought the bongos were too loud; others thought they weren't loud enough. We got so focused on getting the background bongos just right that by the time the commercial was ready to air, we weren't listening too carefully to the lyrics—until the commercial aired nationally during a Saturday morning cartoon.

With the bongo drums blaring, the innocent lyric about fruity marshmallow shapes was gargled and lost under the music. The word "shapes" actually sounded closer to a word that would get most children's mouths washed out with soap. This was an embarrassing and costly mistake. Worse, it was the children viewers who caught it! Letters poured into the cereal company, complaining about the naughty words we were using to sell cereal. Though the error was quickly fixed, we learned the hard way to stay focused on the big picture.

So when witnessing to your audience, ask yourself, *What is my big message?* Which issues should remain in the background? Predestination or salvation? Baptism of the Holy Spirit or the acceptance of Jesus Christ? Keep your focus on how God sent His Son to die for us, not on sticky secondary topics. This strategy will help make Christianity a simple choice for your audience.

TWIST TO OPEN

Many of the most memorable things ever said were simple. The memorable message "twists open" the mind like an easy-open bottle—then sticks there like gum on a shoe. Once stuck, it's almost impossible to remove. Advertising has its share of examples of famous "catch phrases." Who can forget "Got Milk?" That's all you need to say to call to mind any one of the fun, creative commercials in which somebody runs out of milk at an inopportune moment.

The Bible is filled with all kinds of memorable words, too. That's why so many novelists, playwrights and screenwriters have sought inspiration there. John Steinbeck's *The Grapes of Wrath*, Ernest Hemingway's *The Sun Also Rises*, Lillian Hellman's *The Little Foxes*, Robert Heinlein's *Stranger in a Strange Land*, Horton Foote's *Tender Mercies*—these are just a few of the famous titles taken (directly or indirectly) from the Word of God. You, too, can find the stuff in God's Word that makes it user friendly, opening minds and human hearts to God.

"BIG BUTS"

Anyone who works with teens knows it's a constant challenge to get them to open their Bibles. Here's a sure way I found to get them to remember verses that are practical *and* memorable. I call them the "Big But" verses, *but* you might know them as Proverbs chapters 12—15. In most translations, the majority of these verses contain the word "but" in the middle:

Adversity pursues sinners, *but* the righteous will be rewarded with prosperity (Proverbs 13:21).

There is a way which seems right to a man, *but* its end is the way of death (Proverbs 14:12).

I remind teens that if they live according to the Big But verses, they won't end up being "butts" themselves. And it works. Not only do they recall these words of wisdom, but they also remember the meaning behind them.

Quick and Easy Message

Thanks to convenience foods like Hamburger Helper, you can whip up a creamy beef stroganoff in a pinch. Just three easy steps and you're ready to entertain guests. Here are three easy steps for creating a quick message about your faith:

1. Share one simple Bible verse that has impacted your life. For example: "The kindness of God leads you to repentance" (Romans 2:4).
2. Tell your listeners that the verse is for them, too.
3. Remind them that God doesn't take American Express.

EASIER SAID THAN DONE

A simple message is not always simple to create. Usually, the simpler an invention, idea or ad slogan appears, the tougher it was to concoct. Believe me, the mastermind who created "L'eggo my Eggo" was as much a genius as Einstein. Well, sort of. But it takes a lot of time to boil a concept down into a slogan that will stick in your brain longer than you ever wanted it to.

Coming up with a Bible passage that will stick with your audience long after you leave is a challenge, too. Put real time and energy into finding a verse that truly changed your life—one that really turned you on to Christ. Or challenge your audience with a question that's not so simple to answer. For example, "If you don't believe in God, just what do you believe in?"

Remember, the Bible is no different from most TV commercials in that it was written mainly for common folk—the average Joe like you and me. This is not an excuse to set your Bible on a shelf and forget about it, but it's a good reason to remember that the important stuff is also the easiest to understand.

SIMPLE PLEASURES ARE THE BEST

In a world where hundreds of thousands of organizations, products and media outlets are competing for the limited amount of brain space you and I possess, it is crucial that you keep your message simple and focused. So take a lesson from the travails of used-car salesmen: Overselling techniques will usually do more harm than good, especially on the road to heaven. Take time to prepare what you want to say to your audience, then keep it simple and sweet. That way, you will come across not as a religious nut, but as a rational human being who has discovered the abundant goodness of God.

A FINAL KISS

We can sum up this entire chapter with that one memorable acronym: KISS (Keep It Simple, Stupid). Keep that on your lips when witnessing and you just might leave a lasting impression.

Sharing the Bible is not brain surgery; it's much more important than that. So always have a simple message on hand.

Say It in a New Way

You are the salt of the earth; but if the salt has become tasteless, how will it be made salty again? It is good for nothing anymore, except to be thrown out and trampled under foot by men.

MATTHEW 5:13

The shelf life of a product is usually longer than the shelf life of the adjectives used to describe it. No one knows this to be true more than those who worked on a new campaign for the cereal known as the Breakfast of Champions. Wheaties has been around almost as long as breakfast itself; if you think it's hard to get your picture on the front of the box, try coming up with a new way to describe the taste inside.

Since Wheaties are made out of 100% whole wheat, there are only a handful of words that accurately describe the taste. Crispy. Crunchy. Healthy. Hearty. Toasty. Tasty. But after 70 years of use in slogans and jingles, those adjectives have lost their impact; they've become stale to consumers' ears. These words that once had meaning are now of little value. This made describing the taste of Wheaties a real challenge.

The agency's solution was to create a new word, one that captured the hearty personality of Wheaties as well as the taste. A word that would sound fresh and flavorful. One that had all the "oomph!" of the Wheaties heritage.

They had stumbled unexpectedly upon a new word: "Oomph!"

Not only did that never-before-heard word get people to listen, it got America to eat their Wheaties once again.

When advertising something as trivial as cereal flakes, we know the importance of using words that grab the audience's ear. Needless to say, the gospel is much more important than a balanced breakfast.

THE SHELF LIFE OF "CHRISTIAN SPEAK"

Much of the jargon heard in contemporary churches should come with an advisory label: "Best when used before A.D. 67" Just like the words "crispy" and "crunchy," shop-worn phrases like "Jesus saves" and "born-again Christian" have a limited shelf life. A lot of that is because most of us grew up on a steady diet of Christianity in this country. We have heard these expressions all our lives, so they, too, have lost their impact. Instead of gripping the soul as it should, an important question like "Do you know Jesus as your personal Savior?" can go in one ear and out the other.

CHRIST HAD OOMPH!

But it doesn't have to be like this. Christ was confronted with a similar problem. Hounded by the Pharisees, those skeptical legalists who used to infiltrate His gatherings, sowing seeds of discontent among the audience, Jesus knew He had to communicate the truth in a new way—a way that would make the people realize He was the King they had been waiting for. So Jesus referred to Himself as bread, light and the vine. He compared believers to fishers of men, sheep and salt. Christ used colorful parables about fig trees, lost coins and mustard seeds to open the minds of his listeners. In this way, Jesus got His audience to really *hear* what He was saying.

SO WWJD?

We've all seen the bracelets with the enigmatic acronym WWJD, which stands for What Would Jesus Do? Now *there's* a fresh yet simple way to get people to think about Jesus. Now ask yourself, what would Jesus do if He were talking to your audience? He would likely get them to see things in a new way by using a situation familiar to them.

Let's say Jesus was talking to the guy on the highway who just cut you off. He might adapt the story of the Good Samaritan into a tale about "road rage" and a stranded motorist waiting for the auto club. Or, if Jesus were talking to your coworkers, His parable about the unrighteous steward might become a tale about an employee who steals pencils from the supply room. Jesus would pick illustrations that His audience could easily identify with. To say something in a new way doesn't mean saying something completely new; you can make use of illustrations that are 2,000 years old!

TASTES LIKE CHICKEN

If you ever dine at an upscale restaurant where frog legs are on the menu, the maître d' will probably assure you, "It tastes like chicken." And, according to those with more "exotic" tastes, so do rabbit, venison, rattlesnake and turtle. By comparing these wild dishes to something more familiar, our friends get us to try meals we would otherwise avoid.

Why not use that kind of reasoning to get your audience to try the Bible? Cultivate a mind-set that could make their first taste of the Word more inviting. Try referring to the Bible as *The Ultimate Self-Help Book*. After all, regardless of the translation, the Bible contains guidelines for marriage, dating, childrearing, diet, goal setting, finances, stress management. In fact, this book covers every hot topic you've ever seen on daytime talk shows—infidelity, racism, sibling rivalry, jealousy, addictive behavior. All of a sudden, the black leather book seems a lot less scary. People will find in its pages the advice they've always wanted, but didn't know where to look for it.

Um, It Doesn't Taste Like Chicken . . .

Sometimes using a not-so-pleasant comparison can be impactful, especially with an audience who thrives on shock value. Phil can do this better than anyone I know—and he's not in advertising. Phil is a youth pastor in one of the toughest areas of Chicago, and he's not taking any chances that he might bore his teens. Once, Phil got up in front of a roomful of teens and asked, "How many of you like the taste of vomit?" Boy, did that grab their attention! Phil wasn't grossing out the teens just to gross them out. It was Phil's way of getting them to really digest Proverbs 26:11:

> Like a dog that returns to its vomit is a fool who repeats his folly.

Phil's words were fresh and appropriate for teens who flirt with gangs and violence on a regular basis. He made contact.

Break the Rules

Still, people might be hung up on the Bible because to them it's "a book of rules"—rules and laws that have no real purpose, like the one on your mattress tag that says, "Do Not Remove Under Penalty of Law." That was just enough incentive for me to tear mine off; not to find out whether the mattress police would come and I would end up on "Cops," but because no one likes to be told what to do. The Israelites didn't like it and I don't either.

It's natural for people to bristle at the law, which God gave to Moses to show us our need for grace. But if you suspect someone has a particular dislike for rules, then don't mention the rules right away. After all, once Christ came into the picture, He did away with some of the more restrictive rules like not mixing your milk and meat (see Exodus 23:19). If your audience doesn't like rules, don't focus on them. Instead, focus on Christ and the golden rule that governs us all:

> Therefore, however you want people to treat you, so treat them, for this is the Law and the Prophets (Matthew 7:12).

A LITTLE BIT TOO COMFORTABLE?

Food isn't the only product group that needs to freshen up its selling vocabulary. Advertisers of fabric softeners could use a little April freshness, too. In spite of all their persuasiveness, there are still plenty of Americans who use towels that are as rough as sandpaper. I was one of them. Why? Hearing essentially the same message about fabric softeners all my life caused me to tune out the message. I was sick of snuggly softness and words of wisdom from a bear who lives in a dryer. Even though my future husband considered the Downy Ball the greatest invention since the remote control, I couldn't care less.

Then the inevitable happened. I was assigned to work on the account of a brand-name fabric softener. Like it or not, I had to try the stuff. As obvious as it may seem to you, I was shocked by the difference one ounce of biodegradable fabric softening agents made in my laundry. Though fabric softener didn't exactly change my life, I'm surprised now that I waited so long to try it.

People who grew up hearing the Word of God in church can suffer from the same ill effects as someone having heard a life-time of television commercials for fabric softeners. Their hearts might need softening because they have become hardened to the message. Don't wait for them to be forced into a sticky situation—as I was with snuggly softness—to give true, committed Christianity a try. Instead, test drive the creativity God gave you and speak to them words of life.

When you say...	They just might hear...	So why not try...
Born Again Christian	religious fanatic	I'm new and improved
backslider	holy hypocrite	going AWOL (Away WithOut the Lord)
Christ in your heart	Christian cliche	Christ is the heart of my life
salvation	Yeah, right	eternal life insurance policy
Jesus washed away my sins	Not that again	Jesus reformatted my hard drive
nonbeliever	yawn	I believe in God. What do you believe in?
witness	That movie about the Amish, starring Harrison Ford	I'm on the God Squad

MORE WAYS TO STAY FRESH

One of the weirdest products I ever wrote ad copy for was something called "fruit protector." Fruit protector is something caterers and home canners use almost daily. It's a commercial form of pectin that you sprinkle on fresh fruit slices to keep them from turning brown. Because if it doesn't look good, not even the flies will nibble.

So how do you keep your testimony as fresh as your fruit salad? Just sprinkle on a little imagination. Then stand on your head if you have to.

JESUS IS YOUR PIN

Unless you keep your money under your mattress, you have a Personal Identity Number (PIN). And, of course, you keep it in a safe place. You memorize it and use it whenever you need to,

Don't leave earth without Him.

whether to access your money, get groceries or to make deposits to your account. But if you forget your PIN, you'll get nothing.

But with a heavenly PIN, or Personal Inheritance Name, you have access to something much bigger and more useful than an ATM. When describing our Lord to others, try referring to Jesus' name as the ultimate PIN, as described in Acts 4:12:

> And there is salvation in no one else; for there is no other name under heaven that has been given among men, by which we must be saved.

Just like your PIN, if you don't know the name of Jesus, you won't gain access to heaven. If you do not know the name above all names, you won't be able to draw on His strength, His courage or His love. And by keeping that Personal Inheritance Name in a safe place—in your heart—you'll use it and won't lose it.

ABSTAIN FROM "ABSTINENCE"

Ahh, the ever-popular principles of abstinence—popular with parents, maybe, but a distant second to Doritos in appeal to teens. Abstinence is something Ward Cleaver might have talked about with Wally and the Beaver, but it's not part of the preferred vernacular of the pierced-navel crowd. Could there be a cool way to talk about this subject that would make it sound not like a dated concept, but like a topic that is of vital importance to teens today?

While working with a Christian crisis pregnancy center on a presentation to young girls, we came up with a fresh idea: We would present the principles of abstinence as HOPO, an acronym for a memorable piece of plain talk—Hands Off, Pants On. Instead of focusing on religious rules prohibiting premarital sex, we determined to talk about why sex was worth the wait for each young woman.

The girls walked away from that presentation with reasons why they should *want* to keep their pants on, instead of reasons why they *had* to. By encouraging them to say "Hands off God's property!" we emphasized every young lady's value in the eyes of God. These girls would still be responsible for their own actions, but HOPO explained the benefits of abstinence in a way they could grasp.

DUDE-A-RONOMY

Old Testament history is important but sometimes a little trying. If you can make the book of Deuteronomy exciting, you may be ready for a career in advertising.

So how do you do it? I tried referring to Deuteronomy as "Dude-a-ronomy." This gave the book a fresh appeal to my audience. Granted, they were teens whose only exposure to the Old Testament starred Charlton Heston, but this fun approach worked. Instead of old men with beards hanging out with sheep, my group imagined directionless dudes just hanging loose—like B.C. beach bums wandering around in the sand for 40 years. Laid-back attitude, no real rules. They needed God more than they needed sunblock. This "hang loose" analogy got the students to realize why the dudes of Dude-a-ronomy needed structure in their lives. It was a fresh new way to look at Moses and the reasons for the Law.

MORE WAYS TO "SAVE"

Learn a lesson from a coupon clipper: "Save" is a word that's hard to resist. This four-letter word will get you to buy things you would never otherwise think to try, from processed cheese to onion dip. It's also one of the best words to use when sharing Christ. Let your audience know that Christ can save them more than a few cents off their grocery bill. Christ can save their marriage, save their peace of mind, save their self-esteem and, of course, in the long run save them from hell. Now find a coupon that can do all that!

NOT NO-SALT, BUT FRESH SALT

As any french-fry fanatic knows, there's no good substitute for salt. An extra dip in ketchup just won't do the trick. Besides having a taste we crave, salt is a preservative and is essential for life, too. Not only would you die without salt, your beef jerky wouldn't outlast the next ice age without it.

But if you forget to pick up a little packet for your fries, you'll live. If the salt in your testimony is missing or flavorless, that's another story. So replace it with fresh salt that preserves the truth, supplies an essential ingredient for Christian life and has its own unique flavor as well. Or, to state Matthew 5:13 *in a new way*, preserve the truth, but keep it tasty, too.

Chapter 5

Keep It Quick

And He came to the disciples and found them sleeping, and said to
Peter, "So, you men could not keep watch with Me for one hour?"
MATTHEW 26:40

Let's be honest, there's a little bit of Peter in all of us. We can't make it through an episode of "Touched by an Angel" without commercial breaks, let alone sit through a Sunday sermon without checking our watches. We treat like a felon the lady who tries to buy 12 cans of cat food in the 10-items-or-less lane. If a show doesn't grab our attention in the first 30 seconds, we start channel surfing. Why? Our attention spans are forever shrinking. Unlike our ears and feet, the attention span does not continue to grow longer as we grow older.

Call it Murphy Brown's Law: The length of the average attention span is directly proportional to the length of the average sitcom (which is also shrinking to make room for more commercials).

Even commercials are shrinking. Once it was common for commercial spots to be 60 seconds in length; now the same advertisers are jamming their messages into 30 or even 15 seconds to get your attention before you can grab the remote. Talking heads—spokespersons who stand holding the product while rhapsodizing about its benefits—have gone the way of the

Flintstones. Now multiple images and high-tech music are the norm, changing every second (or less) to keep you glued to the tube—all to get you to buy an even faster brand of microwave popcorn.

But as our attention spans keep shrinking, the need for Christ keeps expanding. The world needs Jesus more than ever but doesn't have the patience to receive Him. And He will be returning before we know it. So what are we to do? Keep our message quick.

THE THREE- TO FIVE-SECOND WINDOW

Not all advertising is delivered to you via the TV screen. The mailman delivers a lot of it, too. And, through the use of expensive market research and mailing lists, the stuff in your mailbox has been tailored to *you*—your taste in vacations, your favorite stores, even the credit cards you use. Why do advertisers expend so much money and effort on something so many of us call "junk mail"? Because they know there's a three- to five-second window during which they must capture your attention, to get you to read more about their product. If they fail, that piece of mail is headed for the circular file.

Your testimony has a window no bigger. As a spokesperson for Christ, you have about the same amount of time to snag someone's interest—three to five seconds to turn your audience on to Christ, or turn them off.

Christ didn't waste any time grabbing His audience's attention. His words turned heads, changed hearts, healed the sick, convicted consciences and made many people angry. He didn't babble on about the sins of Babylon. Whatever Christ said, He was quick to make a lasting impression.

RAMBLING VS. RAMBO

If Rambo, Dolby stereo sound and all the special effects in Hollywood can't keep a paying audience captivated for very long, chances are you can't either. I learned this principle from my one-time boss, a former Chicago Ad Woman of the Year.

Regardless of how entertaining our words seemed to me or how many nights we stayed late to work on a commercial, she reminded us that we don't always have the latest computer-generated special effects to grab viewers. And just because the wife doesn't have the remote control in her hands doesn't mean she can't tune us out in her head. Instead of paying close attention to our carefully worded advertising rationale, she could be trying to remember the name of the cute guy who played Potsie* on "Happy Days." So, if we don't keep our message focused and to the point, we could easily lose our audience's attention and, worse, our audience's business.

The same holds true when sharing the gospel. Don't turn your testimony into a marathon event. Remember, a wandering mind is a good place to lose a wandering people. Watch your audience. Make sure you don't turn the exciting into the mundane. And unless you have a cameo appearance by Sylvester Stallone dangling from a helicopter, keep your message to the point.

A SNEAK PREVIEW

Before Hollywood gets your undivided attention in a movie theater, they give you a little taste of what you're in for the next time you go to the movies. They do this with a trailer, or preview of coming attractions. A preview might contain *highlights* of a riotous Julia Roberts comedy or an Arnold Schwarzenegger sci-fi action adventure. Another might provide a *summary* of a

* Anson Williams

romantic epic starring Leonardo DiCaprio. Or a preview might *pose a question* that can only be answered by seeing the new Meryl Streep thriller. No matter how they go about it, previews let you

know what you're buying before you shell out two hours of your time and a whole lot of money for a ticket and a box of jujubes. ("You'll laugh! You'll cry! You'll kiss 10 bucks good-bye!")

Therefore be on the alert, for you do not know which day your Lord is coming (Matthew 24:42).

You can give your audience a preview of Christianity, too—a quick taste just big enough to pique interest. Before you know it, they'll be wanting the full-length feature presentation.

So think, what's the preview you're going to share with others to get blockbuster results? It could contain *highlights* of your testimony:

- "When I'm going through a rough time, I remind myself that God never puts more on my plate than I can handle."
- "God's my only friend who doesn't get mad when I want to talk at 3 A.M."

- "If it weren't for Christ, I'd still judge my worth by the size of my thighs."

Your preview could *summarize* the big picture:

- "The Bible offers you better advice than all the TV talk shows put together."
- "Don't panic. Pray!"
- "Christianity has made life great, and the sequel's supposed to be even better!"
- "You can't rewind your life, but God can erase your mistakes."

Or, you can ask an unforgettable *question*:

- "So where are you spending your eternal vacation?"
- "You know, my faith is the most important thing in my life. May I ask, what's the most important thing in yours?"
- "Hmm. I don't know the answer to that. Why not ask God yourself?"
- "Can I pray for you?"

You might not have special effects or Dolby sound at your disposal, but you *are* talking about the most exciting topic imaginable: our Creator. A little preview can go a long way.

QUICK TO HEAR

An important dead person (whose name I forgot because I wasn't paying attention) once said, "Go into all the world and be a witness for Christ. And if you have to, open your mouth." Truly, the biggest part of witnessing might not be what comes out of your mouth, but what goes into your ears. Think about it for a moment. When you pray, who does most of the talking and who does most of the listening? The greater a person's need, the greater their need to talk. So let them.

One of the most awkward situations I have been in was dealing with a former youth-group member who had walked away from God. I hadn't seen this young lady for a few years and I was both happy and stunned to see her. At first, all I could concentrate on was her pierced tongue. But once she started talking, the pain her tongue went through seemed nothing compared to the pain her heart had experienced. She told me how she had been molested as a child and now had a difficult time trusting men. Seeking love, she ended up in a lesbian relationship. Other areas of her life were equally twisted. Though she had taken many wrong turns, I couldn't think of one verse or passage that seemed right to share at that point. The best thing for me to do was just listen.

Listen, listen, listen. Listen with patience and understanding. Then listen some more. More than you need to capture their attention, your audience needs *your* attention. Whether they're bothered by a serious, life-threatening problem or just a seriously bad hair day before a big date, always be quick to use your ears.

QUICK TO WIGGLE

I stopped listening to my high-school algebra teacher on the second day of class. That's how I perfected the useless art of ear wiggling. Not really caring about logarithms and polynomials, but desperately needing the credit for the course to graduate, I faked listening for an entire school year. While my teacher thought I was concentrating on him, I was really concentrating on how to wiggle my ears. First the left lobe. Then the right. Finally, both together. Of course, my grades at the end of the year clearly showed that I knew a whole lot more about ear wiggling than algebra.

Granted, this carefully cultivated talent doesn't have much practical use, but it will forever remind me of two things: (1) the importance of holding someone's attention and (2) no matter how easy it is to look like you're listening when you're not, it will soon become obvious whether you were paying attention. So be a good listener, not a good wiggler.

TIME IS VALUABLE

Can you think of anything more aggravating than people who waste your time? People who put you on hold. People who are constantly late. Such people make *us* late and raise our blood pressure. Even when you casually witness for Christ, you must remember that time is a valuable commodity. People are busy and if you take too much of their time, they'll tune you out just like the congregation of a pastor who goes over by a half hour.

Sure, nothing in our schedules can compare with the importance of the Word of God, but work *with* your audience's time, not against it. You might need to say just *one thing* to make a working mother think about eternity. Making sure she isn't late for her son's soccer game will speak louder than your willingness to spend another hour telling her about Jesus.

FAST BUT WORTH THE WAIT

Few things are more exciting or memorable than a roller-coaster ride—and few things are more boring than waiting in line for the roller coaster. If the ride is any good, the line will be at least two hours and yet the ride itself lasts only a few minutes. Still, screaming at the top of your lungs while you think you're going to hurl is so much fun that you stand in line again. Years later, you will still remember the thrill of the ride, not the monotony of standing in line.

Your message should be just like a roller-coaster ride—fast, memorable and well worth the wait. Nausea is optional, but not recommended. Your testimony may last for a few brief moments, but hopefully it will stick with your audience a lifetime. Remember, you can't measure the lasting effects of what you said by the length of time you took to say it.

IN SHORT . . .

Quick, think of everything you know about God. You didn't learn it in one sermon. You didn't understand it all one Sunday morning. You've picked up chunks here and there. There is nothing wrong with breaking up your testimony into bite-size pieces, so don't confuse a fast testimony with fast answers.

> So shall My word be which goes forth from My mouth;
> it shall not return to Me empty, without accomplishing
> what I desire (Isaiah 55:11).

Keeping your testimony quick is like dropping a bomb behind enemy lines: You want to get in and out of there fast. If your mission is a success, someone will see results. The Word of God will not come back void, even if you never get to see the harvest.

But saying something quickly opens the door for you to follow up with your audience. You can ask about an issue or struggle you've prayed about. You can give them a Scripture reference that addresses whatever they're dealing with. You can take time to listen patiently to the temporary insanity they are experiencing. Be attentive to your audience's needs and you will keep them captivated, not captured.

And always leave them wanting more.

Don't Expect Overnight Results

I planted, Apollos watered, but God was causing the growth.
THE APOSTLE PAUL, 1 CORINTHIANS 3:6

Ho, Ho, Ho!
THE JOLLY GREEN GIANT

Only in advertising do things magically grow overnight. The Chia Pet, for example. For the two of you out there unfamiliar with this breed, the Chia is half animal, half plant and usually hibernates till the Christmas shopping season. When cared for correctly, the Chia figurine sprouts a fuzzy growth that looks more like clover than fur. In the TV commercial, an actress rubs a seed paste all over the Chia and within 30 seconds, a Chia coat appears.

But the reality is much different. The amazing growth you see on TV doesn't happen when you get the Chia home. You wait and wait and wait and still your Chia Pet looks like it has Chia mange. And if by chance it does grow, by next Christmas your figurine will be in need of Chia Rogaine.

Then there's the larger-than-life growth experienced in the Valley of the Jolly Green Giant. You know the guy. He's rather large, not the best dresser, reminds you of genetically engineered brussels sprouts. His hills are the greenest green, and his corn is high as an elephant's . . . well, you get the picture. You have no idea where this valley is, let alone what the giant uses for fertilizer. Still, the Jolly Green Giant and his crop are impressive, so you buy his frozen corn niblets and boil them in the bag for five minutes. It's the perfect side dish for those who are domestically challenged like myself.

Advertising promotes a warped view of overnight wonders, from time-lapse photography of Chia fuzz and Just For Men hair coloring to the effortless farming of a green giant. Ironically, advertisers know not to expect overnight results when trying to convince you of anything—which frosting is creamier, which spaghetti sauce is chunkier, even which deodorant stick keeps you drier. Advertisers know it can take several Christmas seasons of seeing that Chia before you actually buy one.

Give me millions of dollars to buy media time, the latest in special effects, a bite and a smile from Michael Jordan and I still can't get you to try a product before the coupon expires. Yet when it comes to sharing the good news of Jesus Christ, I, like anyone else, expect Jack and the Beanstalk-type results.

Hey, we all know that the decision to become a Christian is a big one. It's more important and longer lasting than a Chia Pet, wheat flakes or anything else you'll see advertised on TV. So instead of expecting an instant conversion, allow the Holy Spirit time to water and germinate the seed you've planted.

MIRACLE GRO IS NOT A CHRISTIAN PRODUCT

Wouldn't it be great if there were a special fertilizer you could spread over somebody to turn them into a strong believer? Well, there is. It's called *time*. The Holy Spirit was very liberal with how much He used on me. It took me more than half my life to take root and grow to this point—and I still need constant pruning!

We've all been touched and blessed by incredibly dramatic conversion stories, but for the most part they are the exception, not the rule. In this spiritual climate, you'll find it takes patience, hard work and lots of faith to see growth from the seeds you've planted in nonbelievers. Or as the Jolly Green Giant might say, "Hoe, hoe, hoe!"

In the spring of 1996, I had the opportunity to hoe where few Christians have hoed before: China. I traveled there with a church group with plans to care for children in an orphanage. Little did we know that our stay would be as spicy as the moo-shoo chicken.

The fun started the day we arrived in Beijing. Chinese government officials were skeptical of any Americans who wanted to help their orphans, so our plans were derailed by our own good intentions. Actually, God had a different field for us to farm, that being the ancient city of Kaifeng. (Don't worry, I had never heard of it either.)

Though only 12 hours by train from Beijing, Kaifeng is 12 light-years from reality. Not one person there has ever *heard* of McDonald's. And everyone was Chinese. Everyone, that is, except our group of assorted Americans—three blondes, three tall white guys, one African-American female and our very own teenage deviant.

We stood out in Kaifeng like, well, 10 Americans in Kaifeng. Instead of working in an orphanage, however, we were blessed with the opportunity to help at a school for disabled children. Not only did we make friends with the students and teachers, we gained the trust of many public officials, paving the way for future mission workers. Though we will never see the fruits of our labors, we know that someday, someone will—on God's timetable, not ours.

CALL BEFORE MIDNIGHT TONIGHT!

This is a tough one. The rule of thumb is if you've got to call before midnight to get a product, chances are it won't be around next month. Like that amazing wok you bought from that guy on the slickly produced infomercial: You used the wok a few times until you heard about his new, improved sandwich maker; now both are gathering dust in your basement.

Generally, companies whose products will stand the test of time don't need to employ "act now" sales techniques. Jesus has certainly stood the test of time—He was there at the beginning (see John 1:1) and He's still going strong. And since salvation is not a fly-by-night offer, why pressure your audience as if it were?

The problem is that no one really knows when Christ will return and our time will run out (see Mark 13:32). And even if God is still accepting calls tomorrow, not one of us is guaranteed that we will be here then to make that all-important call (see James 14:14).

Always emphasize the quality of what you're offering, but watch your audience's response carefully. If they are nearing a decision but want to put it off until tomorrow, gently remind them that eternal life is a limited-time offer.

DRIVEN TO MAKE A SALE

High-pressure sales techniques will usually bomb, whether you're talking about First Corinthians or rich Corinthian leather. That's what I learned when shopping for a car.

Chicago is a city teeming with public transportation, so it was very easy for me to live there for years without a car. But the time finally came for me to trade my walking shoes for a pair of fuzzy dice. I wasn't sure what I was looking for in a car except three things: (1) I wanted a vehicle that would fit my *lifestyle*; (2) I wanted a brand with a *trustworthy name* and (3) I wanted to buy it at a dealer where they'd throw in the the mats for free. Having been out of the car market for more than a decade, I had no idea how expensive cars had become. The last car I priced had been a brand-new 1976 Vega on "The Price is Right," but car prices nowadays begin near the top of "The $25,000 Pyramid." So when I started browsing dealerships, I decided to allow myself several weeks before committing to a transaction.

While test driving new cars was often fun, the ubiquitous salesmen made my search a headache. Many would pressure me to buy before I left their showrooms. Others thought they knew my needs better than I did.

There's no need to come across like a fast-talking salesman when pitching the gospel. What you're "selling" will not disappoint "buyers" once they get it home.

After weeks of searching, I finally found a car that I liked with a dealer I trusted. No fast talk. No breathing down my neck. Instead, this dealer let me examine the car for as long as I wanted without pressuring me to sign anything. Even though I was confident that I would buy a car from him when I left his showroom, I did not make my purchase on that day; I was determined not to make a hasty decision. After all, a car is a big commitment, not an impulse buy. A few days later, I returned to purchase that same car from the dealer—and my mother bought one, too!

Obviously, one's decision to accept Christ is far more serious than buying a car; it's the biggest commitment a person can make. This decision affects every part of your lifestyle, requiring you to trust completely in His name. Fortunately, the offer comes with an outstanding lifetime guarantee (see Deuteronomy 31:6 and Ephesians 1:13,14, among others).

So when you share your faith, remember, you don't need to resort to high-pressure sales tactics. *What you have is what they want.* Allow your audience at least as much time as you would allow yourself to weigh the benefits of leather vs. vinyl seats.

FISHERS OF MEN, NOT SEA MONKEYS

Christ has called us to be fishers of men (see Matthew 4:19). But what you end up with in your net isn't always what you imagined when you first went fishing. Consider for a moment those strange creatures you see advertised in comic books: Sea Monkeys. (They don't look like monkeys at all—more like the Sea Grinch who stole Christmas).

Sometime between the puppy that got run over by a car and the turtle that was lost and later found shriveled behind our television set, I was the not-so-proud owner of a sea kingdom. The foil pouch in which the Sea Monkeys came featured a cartoon illustration of king and queen sea monkeys swimming in front of a castle, surrounded by their simian sea babies. I dumped the contents of the pouch into a bowlful of water according to the instructions, fully expecting to wake up the next morning to the wondrous sight of my very own monkey village. But instead of sea royalty, all I found in my fishbowl were a bunch of squirmy things barely visible to the naked eye. Bitterly disappointed, I did what any Sea Monkey pet owner would do—and no doubt has done—I flushed them down the toilet.

Learn a lesson from those Sea Monkeys: What you expect to catch and what you are *expected* to catch are two different things. The friend you brought to Bible study might not be ready to become a church member for a while. Another friend who's willing to pray with you might not be ready to give up smoking. But that's OK. If overnight growth is too much to expect for brine shrimp, don't expect it from your audience. It's better to reel in an agape guppy than to forever talk about the big one who got away.

INSTANT LOSER

The only way to lose 10 pounds of weight instantly is to cut off your head. Weight loss, as many of us have learned the hard way, does not happen overnight. Still, millions of Americans buy the milk shakes and the treadmills that eventually disappear beneath piles of clothes in our bedrooms. That piece of dry toast and half a grapefruit soon become appetizers for an Extra Value Meal #3.

Change takes time, whether it's shedding unwanted chins or unwanted sin. The Bible reminds us that Christianity is an ongoing journey. In other words, you will never meet your ultimate goal until the final spiritual weigh-in. And yet you "press on toward the goal for the prize of the upward call of God in Christ Jesus" (Philippians 3:14).

So be as patient with your audience as God has been with you.

A 30-DAY TRIAL PERIOD

Experts tells us it takes only three weeks to make or break a habit. So take heart. In 30 days, any one of these positive actions could become a healthy habit for that person you recently brought to Christ. You probably can think of more:

- Have daily devotions.
- Join a Bible study.
- Pray regularly.
- Stomp out a negative habit.
- Start each morning by reading a chapter of Proverbs.
- Discover one new thing about Christ every day.

INSTANT BREAKFASTS, NOT INSTANT CHRISTIANS

If I know that it can take years for me to change your mind about something as trivial as cereal flakes—even with the help of media specialists, a research department, product testing, intensive market analysis and the endorsement of a super athlete—then I must be realistic about my ability to get people to change their beliefs about Christ.

It took more than 20 years to change mine.

No, I am not a Chia Christian who blossomed overnight or a jolly green spiritual giant. Of those responsible for leading me to my decision to accept Christ, many might not even remember my name. My resident hall assistant in college. The youth leader who gave me a ride home. A stranger who prayed for me in passing. The assistant pastor who chuckled instead of scolding me for listening to the World Series during a Sunday night service. Thanks to their combined efforts, seeds took root in my life.

Be realistic about what you can do vs. the results you will see. The seeds whose crop you harvest now were sowed by others. Someone else will have the joy of harvesting yours.

Chapter 7

Last but Not Least: Just Do It

But be doers of the word, and not hearers only.
JAMES 1:22, NKJV

Back in the days of old, before there were super athletes with multimillion dollar NBA contracts, kids bought shoes for one reason only: the decoder ring. At least that was true for me. One year, my family was soon to depart for a trip to New York City, so my dad took me to the shoe store to buy some comfortable walking shoes. Thanks to another pushy salesman, I tried on every kind of shoe imaginable—penny loafers, Hush Puppies, the ever-popular saddle shoe. But instead of picking a pair that agreed with my feet, I picked the pair that gave me the decoder ring to go with my blisters: a pair of one-size-too-small Buster Browns.

Now, the Buster Brown decoder ring was well worth any pain the shoes caused my feet. For starters, the ring gave you the ability to crack secret codes (a must for a six-year-old). But that's not all! The decoder ring had its very own magnifying glass for frying innocent bugs (another must for a six-year-old), plus a secret compartment big enough to store them in.

So I got the Buster Brown shoes and decoder ring, a subject that would remain a sore spot with my dad for much longer than the shoes would stay on my feet. For once we arrived in New York, we spent a good chunk of our vacation searching for a comfortable pair of Red Ball Jets.

FROM BUSTER BROWN TO NIKETOWN

But that was then. Nowadays, athletic shoes rule. Instead of a little decoder ring, every shoe comes with its own superstar endorsement and gazillion-dollar ad campaign. (I can barely recall a commercial for Buster Browns.) More often than not, today's shoe commercials are more entertaining than the games they interrupt. They make me, the ultimate couch potato, actually consider exercising something other than my fingers on the remote control.

So before long, I find myself in NikeTown, a wondrous place that's half shoe store, half sports shrine, located in downtown Chicago. There I'm greeted by TV monitors showing inspirational video footage of Nike athletes on the field, on the course, on the court and in the lanes; decorative basketball hoops; retired shoes of retired athletes and other cool stuff that makes me proud to be a consumer. I make a beeline for the shoe department where I'm helped by someone really important—no, not Michael, Bo or Tiger, but a scrawny high-school kid who doesn't judge me for my supersized toes or pressure me to buy anything. He just offers me a shoe horn and a footlet. Not only do I leave NikeTown with a brand-new pair of cross trainers, but a Nike T-shirt, too, making me their one billionth human billboard.

Think for a moment about all that's involved these days in getting someone to buy a shoe—a 100% synthetic, soon-to-be-stinky-with-a-worn-down-heel shoe.

Well, here's news for you. Whether you're telling people about high-tops or the Word of God, expect a lot of work to go into the process and a lot of people, too. Although a superstar athlete might get the credit for turning me on to the athletic shoe *du jour*, it was a 17-year-old kid making minimum wage who saw to it that I walked out wearing them. It took the combined efforts of lots of regular, unheralded people to get me to buy their product. And not one of them was on a street corner with a megaphone condemning me for not exercising.

The day those advertisers are not in your face will be the day their shoes are not on your feet.

Just like selling shoes, witnessing is a team effort—lots of people focusing on the goodness of God. Romans 12:4 reminds us, "We have many members in one body and all the members do not have the same function." It takes a team of people to get one person to come to Christ. All you have to do is your part.

FOUR GOSPELS, FOUR REGULAR GUYS

God wants you to be a doer of the word, not a hearer only (see James 1:22). And there's a lot to be done. But the good news is you don't need to be a super athlete to do your part. You just have to be yourself and you have to be willing.

Consider the Gospels and the men wrote them—just four real guys who really loved the Lord: Matthew was a tax collector, not much different from the guy from H&R Block who helps you with your returns; Mark wrote his gospel account like a news reporter sticking to the facts; Luke was a no-nonsense doctor; then there was the blue-collar flavor of John, a local fisherman.

Notice that not one of the Gospels was written by a Maytag repairman. If you want to be used by God, you should know you won't be sitting around with time on your hands.

Doing Your Part

Have you ever been tempted to be a spiritual slacker and let someone else do the work? Not a good idea. Take a lesson from Jonah about blowing off the work you're supposed to be doing for God. Jonah ended up spending three not-so-luxurious days and nights in "whale jail." Who knows how Jonah would be remembered today if he had gone to Nineveh straightaway and done the work God called him to do? Jonah might be known as one of the Bible's great fishers of men, not the catch of the day.

Who knows what catch God has in mind for you? So procrastinate when it comes to mowing the lawn, but don't put off doing your part for God. You don't know who God has put in your path today.

Holding Your Testimony Together

Did you know a baseball has 216 stitches? It takes each and every one to hold those two pieces of cowhide (formerly horsehide) together when the ball is whacked by Sammy Sosa. In the same way, all the numerous little things *you* do help communicate the message of the gospel to a nonbeliever. An act of kindness, your smile, sharing a helpful proverb—these things help stitch together a sincere picture of Jesus. If you're not modeling Christ, you're just another knuckleball.

DO IT BECAUSE YOU WANT TO, NOT BECAUSE YOU HAVE TO

But as for you, brethren, do not grow weary of doing good.

2 THESSALONIANS 3:13

One of my most memorable advertising assignments was to write a radio spot selling body dismemberment insurance to teachers in New Jersey. (Hey, I don't make up the assignments, I just do the work. Believe me, there are better things to write about than losing a finger in wood shop.)

Obviously, not every work assignment is a winner, but every assignment from God is. Sharing Christ is a lot more fun than writing the stuff kids read on the back of a cereal box while their flakes get soggy. Witnessing makes me tick and it should make you tick, too. But if doing God's work seems like a fate worse than losing a finger in wood shop, maybe *you* are the one God is concerned about. Growing weary of doing good is not a good sign. So find a fresh, new way to share God's love, then be sure to share it with yourself.

MORE CROSS-TRAINING: STEPPING OUT OF YOUR COMFORT ZONE

Be strong and courageous! Do not tremble or be dismayed, for the LORD your God is with you wherever you go.

JOSHUA 1:9

To work in advertising requires stepping out of your comfort zone; that's where all of the good ideas are found. That's why advertising agencies strive to create environments where you won't be "chicken" to express any idea, even if that idea requires you to dress like a chicken.

I was at a client meeting where a fellow writer showed up wearing a chicken suit. No power tie or wing tips; just yellow tights and lots of feathers. The writer's willingness to dress up like a chicken led to a successful campaign for the client. But he never would've worn the chicken suit if he thought for a moment everyone would laugh *at* him instead of *with* him. With his chicken legs and unplucked feathers, my coworker was comfortable in the meeting. (His commute home was another story.)

Advertising agencies aren't the only ones who want their workers to step out of their comfort zones. So does God. No, you probably won't be required to wear a chicken suit; just be willing to go where God wants you to go. Psalm 91:4 promises you'll be under the protection of His wings, so go for it!

Heinz 57 Steak Sauce wouldn't be what it is without all 57 ingredients. Without you, a nonbeliever might never experience Christ. Remember, the impact you make on that one life is like that dash of onion in the steak sauce: You can't do it on your own, but your contribution is crucial.

I experienced the thrill of my life a few years back when I got a call from my pastor asking me to step out of my comfort zone. He asked me to accompany him and his daughter on a weeklong mission trip to Sicily. Good-bye, Hamburger Helper. Hello, linguini!

Naturally, I jumped at the opportunity, but if I had had any clue as to what I was getting into, I may never have bothered packing my bags. I was expecting comfortable, pasta-filled fellowship in a beautiful, even romantic, setting. God had something else in mind.

After arriving at the airport in Catania, Sicily, we were picked up by the missionaries who invited us. The scenic drive from the airport was incredible—mountains and winding roads, like pages torn from a travel magazine. Still, as we passed a local dump, I couldn't help but notice the gigantic tents pitched on the premises. I was stunned. I commented to one of the missionaries, "Gee, I was expecting Sicily to be poor, but there are people sleeping in tents in the dump."

The missionary chuckled at my comment, then replied, "Oh, those aren't Sicilians who live in the dump. That's where *we* stay!"

Sure enough, in the middle of the town dump, the missionaries had set up a big tent mission; it was the cheapest place in Catania where they could rent space for a temporary outreach. But the missionaries had converted the dump into holy ground. There were sleeping tents, kitchen tents, shower areas, even plumbing. And every night in the middle of rusty car parts and old tires, they held an evangelistic meeting. Lives were changed in Sicily, including mine.

Granted, a trip to the dump in Sicily isn't for everyone, and sharing Christ with a neighbor at Kmart can be just as rewarding. The key thing is to be willing to step into new territory for Christ, even if it's in your own backyard.

. . . AND REPEAT

Repetition isn't only important when doing tummy tucks. Repetition is also vital to the success of your message. So say it again. You can't repeat it too many times. In other words, repeating your message is not a bad idea. At the risk of sounding redundant, what I am trying to say is that saying the same thing over and over makes your message more effective. Got it?

You wouldn't remember every detail of your favorite "Brady Bunch" episode if you hadn't seen it in reruns 14 times. So don't be afraid to rerun your message with your audience. And don't be afraid to reread that last paragraph, either.

AVOID THE MISTAKES OF PHONE SOLICITORS

When dinner rolls around, there's only one thing you want—and it's not a phone call. Remember, timing is everything, even when sharing something as important as God. Make sure that the people you are sharing with are ready to hear what you have to say. If they have something they feel is more urgent to discuss, or they're trying to watch the big game, be sensitive to their needs. As trivial as that may sound, these things can make a well-intended message as welcome as the phone ringing when you're trying to pass the potatoes.

NOW GIMME THAT GOSPA!

"Go into all the world and preach the gospel to all creation."
MARK 16:15

Good salesmen have a few things in common. For starters, they know a sale is accomplished through a *series* of calls—one to get to know the customer, another to understand his need and additional calls because building a long-term relationship is key. Salesmen are also big on breath mints.

But the best salespeople go a step further. They live by the GOSPA, that being an acronym for Goal, Objective, Strategy, Plan and Action. It's a great tool for figuring out how you can reach any audience. So think, what's your GOSPA for sharing Christ?

MY LONG-TERM GOAL IS . . .

. . . that someday my new neighbor will experience Christ.

MY SHORT-TERM OBJECTIVE IS . . .

. . . to interact with her daily to build a sincere relationship.

MY STRATEGY IS . . .

. . . to let her experience Christlike love through my Christlike actions.

MY PLAN IS . . .

. . . to help her with little tasks.

THE ACTION I AM TAKING NOW IS . . .

. . . to take her kids to soccer practice.

JUST DO IT.

So learn a lesson from Nike: It takes a lot of people to effectively witness to a single individual. People who make you want something without ever insisting you need it. People you aspire to be like, who communicate in ways that are always exciting and fresh. And, for the most part, they are regular people just like you and me.

Think of the ads you like and what makes you buy the things you do. Then use that kind of thinking and do your part to talk about God to your friends. It's easier than it sounds. Christianity shouldn't sound as stilted and contrived as an infomercial. Simply make them want it.

A CHECKLIST OF DO'S AND DON'TS

- DO be yourself.

- DO be prepared.

- DO remember that you are talking about the most exciting topic out there.

- DO focus on God's love, not His wrath.

- DON'T get defensive.

- DON'T get discouraged.

- DON'T expect someone else to pinch-hit for you.

- DON'T be afraid. You have nothing to lose. Your audience, on the other hand, has a lot at stake.

PART II

BUT WAIT— THERE'S MORE!

Creating a Commercial for Your Faith

But if we walk in the light as He Himself is in the light,
we have fellowship with one another, and the blood of Jesus
His Son cleanses us from all sin.

1 JOHN 1:7

Have you ever had a stain on your carpet or kitchen counter for so long that you couldn't remember if the offending substance was animal, vegetable or mineral? You're not alone. Cleaning is hard work, even with the simplest of stains, and it often takes more than elbow grease to do the job. That's why so much of your grocer's shelf space is devoted to cleaning products that make your life easier and leave a lovely pine scent.

But if you think cleaning is hard work, try writing a commercial that makes toilet bowl stains look both disgusting *and* appealing. One such project I worked on featured not a spokesman for the cleaning product, but a spokes*pig*. A nervous spokespig. A pig who was suffering an anxiety attack because his beloved world of filth was coming to an end.

The commercial started with the spokespig racing across a freshly mopped floor, screaming, "Hey! Hey! Hey! What happened to my pigpen? This place is supposed to be dirty!" Where was all the scum and filth he loved to wallow in? He couldn't bear to say good-bye to his germ-ridden home. After all, what's this world coming to if a pig can't be a pig? As much fun as this commercial was, it ended up dying in consumer testing and the spokespig ended up as bacon.

Did you know that the average family uses 13 different cleaning products to eradicate dust and grime and keep their home free of unpleasant odors? Stain removers, wood polishes, specialty surface cleaners, nonabrasive scrubbing powders, plug-in country-fresh air deodorizers. But for getting rid of sin in your life, you need only one proven Stain Fighter:

And now why do you delay? Arise, and be baptized, and wash away your sins, calling on His name (Acts 22:16).

NO STAIN TOO TOUGH

Once a coworker was shooting a commercial for an industrial-strength cleanser for which the client brought in his own "stain specialist." No, it wasn't the guy who spilled grape juice on your new carpeting, but a researcher who specialized in creating stains on sinks and counters which this product would then miraculously remove. The funny thing was the specialist couldn't get any of his substances to stain convincingly! Finally, the director sent a production assistant to buy a batch of plain, old blueberries. That did the trick.

The worst mess I ever had to deal with wasn't on a sound stage but in my parents' bathroom. I was home from college for

Christmas break, trying to catch some z's when my little sister woke me up and said, "Ginger, the toilet's making weird noises." Yeah, whatever. Jiggle the handle. "No," she insisted, "it's really acting weird!" Before long, I heard it. *Vroom. Vroom.* So I got up and sure enough, the toilet was vrooming. Not only that, but steam was coming out of the bowl, too. Suddenly, the entire thing blew up! Porcelain pelted the wall and you-know-what hit the fan.

Luckily, we weren't hurt. Come to find out, the explosion was caused by an overheating water heater. The hot water had backed up into the toilet tank, turning it into a pressure cooker when we flushed. Where's Mr. Clean when you need him?

HOW DID CHRIST CLEAN UP YOUR LIFE?

Spokespigs, tough stains and toilet explosions. Advertising has perfected all kinds of ways to demonstrate how a product can clean up the mess these things leave. Your testimony is like a commercial demonstrating the cleansing power of Jesus Christ, and if people are impressed by the cleansing power of a lemon-scented detergent, wait till they get a load of the power of the blood of Christ!

Sharing with others what Christ did for you is your testimony. Sometimes a testimony can be dramatic like a toilet explosion. Or it may be the story of how you were set free from a compulsive sin that marked your life like a stubborn blueberry stain. Or maybe you're just experiencing an overall difference in your world, like the spokespig. Let me give you a few examples.

FROM DIRTY PIG TO SPIC AND SPAN

Can anything good come out of Southern California? Imagine growing up there as a wild surfer whose only experiences with church left the bitter aftertaste of religion or were just plain confusing, like heavy-metal music blasting from the sound system of the Crystal Cathedral. That's the story of Rusty.*

Growing up in a family that feared God, Rusty went to church on a regular basis as a child. Unfortunately, theirs was a church where God was a religion, not a reality. People there were surface cleaners, never taking off their protective gloves to let God's cleansing power reach inside their lives to work on what really needed cleaning. So, as Rusty grew older, he walked away from church and Sunday morning became a time for surfing and sun.

But as the Bible promises, the Word of God does not return void. Years later, when Rusty moved to the Midwest, he still had an unsatisfied hunger for God. And he knew inside it was time to end his spiritual fast.

I thought Rusty was sort of cute, so I decided to invite him to church. Knowing how Rusty felt about religion, I was choosy about the kind of church that would be right for him. I had three in mind—all churches I loved for different reasons.

The first was a church that I affectionately call Yuppies for Jesus, where the majority of the members are single, upscale Christians who work in downtown Chicago. The second was a sub-urban megachurch, with its supersized sanctuary, gymnasium, cafeteria and giant video projection screen. The third, being my home church, was a mishmash of street people, diverse cultures and families who provided me with spiritual support. After much prayer, I brought Rusty to mine, although I was paranoid that he would be turned off by the unique smell that can only be described as a combination of old hymnals, Old Spice and baby burp.

This church really touched his heart. He was not only moved by the sermon, but by the people as well. There he found the taste of God he had always craved. Before long, it was Rusty who was hounding *me* to go to church.

* Rusty is not his real name. Nobody's real name is Rusty.

Little by little, Rusty grew into an awesome man of God. He would say, "Church is to my soul what scratching is to my mosquito bites. I always knew it would feel good, but not this good. Now I can't get enough!" Rusty is still growing strong in the Lord today.

SPARKLES LIKE NEW

Wash me thoroughly from my iniquity, and cleanse me from my sin.
PSALM 51:2

Can you imagine a cleansing power that works so thoroughly that it makes even the oldest, dingiest, filthiest item sparkle like new? Well, don't limit your imagination to Windex.

Once I joined a friend who was taking a class in Christian counseling at a prominent suburban church. The class sounded interesting enough, but I've got to tell you, I was a bit skeptical when the teacher walked in. She immediately brought to mind the stereotypical Sunday School teacher who has lived in a protective "Christian bubble" all her life. A bun on her head, a big smile and a soft, sweet voice that never dared utter a four-letter word.

She started her teaching about counseling people in dire need by telling a story that had all the makings of a made-for-TV miniseries starring Valerie Bertinelli. "Imagine being a young girl not knowing the real meaning of love. You grew up in a home where you were molested as a child. Your drunk father beat you . . . your boyfriend raped you . . . you ran away. . . ." On and on she went. "You got divorced . . . started drinking." I rolled my eyes. *What would this lady know about counseling someone like that? Give me a break.* Then she continued, "That young girl was me."

I was floored. Actually, I was embarrassed at myself. There was no residue of her past on her; it had been completely washed away. No sin is too dirty. Jesus can truly clean up any life and restore any person.

Removes Dirt That You Can See, as Well as Dirt You Can't!

Sometimes, like when faced with blueberry stains, we are plagued by one stubborn sin that just won't seem to budge. It may be smoking, swearing, gossiping, even stealing paper clips from the supply room. Other times, it's what the world can't see that's really dangerous, like dirt you sweep under the carpet.

At a large inner-city church I attended in Chicago, there was an usher who was a closet alcoholic. For a while, he was able to conceal his problem, confining it to that hidden portion of his life that no one else could see. But the problem grew worse and eventually he was bringing his little flask to the weekly services. While sneaking a swig between services one Sunday, the usher's worst nightmare became reality. He dropped the glass flask, smashing it to pieces in the middle of the church lobby. He couldn't hide his problem any longer; everyone knew his secret sin. However, instead of condemning him, the church started an Oil and Wine Ministry for men and women with drinking problems. As far as I know, that ministry still exists today.

So if you think your sins can go unchecked and unnoticed, remember this WARNING: "You have sinned against the LORD, and be sure your sin will find you out" (Numbers 32:23).

More Dramatic Cleansing Action

I have had the privilege of hearing testimonies from participants of a program in Chicago called Teen Challenge. This particular Teen Challenge was a drug-treatment program for young ladies, helping them to overcome their addictions through the power of Christ, and every participant had a dramatic testimony. All had prostituted their bodies; many had spent time in jail; some had even lost their children, casualties of their battle with drugs. And each lady had prayed at one time or another that she would die.

But thanks to the Teen Challenge program, these women experienced Christ's power in full strength. He wiped out addictions and other horrific pain in their lives. He didn't leave any scum, either. Just big smiles. When these women shared their stories, I couldn't help but cry. Their testimonies of salvation dramatically showed the awesome depth and power of God's love.

EVERYDAY CLEAN

But face it. Most of us are not former drug addicts or convicted felons. You probably live in suburbia and floss daily. You might have a few skeletons in your closet but not an entire captivating crypt. That doesn't make your personal testimony any less effective. Actually it might make it more so.

Did you know that when advertising cleaning products, showing an everyday use of an all-purpose cleanser can be more effective than showing a cleaning

I JOHN
1:7
ALL-PURPOSE
CLEANER
WIPES
OUT SIN
100%

Strong enough for a man, but safe enough for a child. The blood of Christ removes addictions, fear, stress, hatred and more! "It is a terrifying thing to fall into the hands of the living God" (Hebrews 10:31), so clean up your act now!

job that's sensational? The removal of ordinary bathtub scum can be more persuasive than showing the Ty-D-Bol man cleaning up the sewers of Toledo. Research tells us this all the time. Why? People respond to what they can relate to. The same is true for the everyday, "regular guy" testimony. Just how *is* Jesus Christ a big part of your life?

Take the story of my oldest sister, Diane. Diane has been a strong follower of Christ all her life. No heroin addiction, no police record, no guest appearances on "The Jerry Springer Show." As a matter of fact, Diane was my polar opposite. While I was sneaking out my bedroom window, Diane was doing her devotions. While I was breaking the legs of my little sister's Barbie dolls, Diane was on her way to youth group. While I was partying hard at college, Diane was studying hard to be a pharmacist.

Now, years later, Diane works with kids with cancer. She is a pharmacist in a children's cancer clinic, where prescribing medicine is the easy part. Not only does Diane draw strength and courage from the Lord to get through each day, He gives her enough to share with the parents of sick children, too. Now *that's* a powerful testimony. And I never complain to Diane about having a lousy day at work.

DON'T JUST GIVE A TESTIMONY, LIVE A TESTIMONY

I beseech you therefore, brethren, by the mercies of God, that you present your bodies a living sacrifice, holy, acceptable to God, which is your reasonable service.
ROMANS 12:1, *NKJV*

My pastor says, "It's better to be a living testimony than a dead one." It's the little things you do every day that will make a big difference to the nonbeliever: your attitude, your joy, being kind to your neighbor's yelping poodle instead of kicking it, volunteering to clean the restroom you complain about at church. Eyes *are* watching you and they're watching you much more closely than any TV commercial.

Christ's life was the ultimate testimony: He healed; He loved children with runny noses; He hung out with people who didn't smell zestfully clean. His testimony was His prayer life, His compassion, His immovable resistance to temptation. Then He allowed Himself to be nailed to a cross for losers like us. Now, 2,000 years later, millions follow Him. Remember, sharing your verbal testimony is important, but nothing speaks as loudly as loving actions.

So demonstrate Christ's power by visibly enjoying how Jesus makes your every day sparkle. If only selling cleansers was this easy.

SHOUT IT OUT!

Whether it's a big nasty spot or just a little mark, all sin stains the same. The good news is Christ can remove all of it. And by applying unconditional love to any situation, you can do more good than an overnight presoak. So stay clear of harsh methods when bringing someone to the Lord. After all, as Romans 2:4 reminds us, it's the goodness of God that causes man to repent.

REVIEW AND REWIND

1. How did Christ clean up your life?

2. What is the best way to demonstrate it?
   a. Before-and-after testimony.
   b. Focus on one stubborn sin.
   c. Dramatic cleansing action.
   d. Dealing with the daily grime.

Shopping for a Religion: Life in the Express Lane

My mother taught me many important things, including never to go grocery shopping on an empty stomach. "If you do," she warned, "you'll buy too much—half of it you don't really need." That's especially easy to do when I run up against The Great Wall of Cereal on aisle 2, where more than 200 brands are beckoning my taste buds, from industrial-strength bran fiber to oatmeal with hatching dinosaur eggs. Then there's the sausage lady who's giving away free samples near the freezer case. Pizza bites, smoky links— I'm not choosy when I'm starving. Finally I ask the stock boy to help me find my favorite vegetable, candy corn, which I nibble on while waiting in line. By the time I leave the store, not only have I spent my entire paycheck, but I'm stuffed like a Thanksgiving turkey. And to think all I came in for was some toilet paper.

SHOPPING FOR A RELIGION IS NO DIFFERENT

My mother's advice doesn't hold true for grocery shopping only. These days, people are spiritually hungry and will throw just about anything into their shopping cart of beliefs. This is something that Paul warned us about: "The Spirit explicitly says that in later times some will fall away from the faith, paying attention to deceitful spirits and doctrines of demons" (1 Timothy 4:1). If only people were as choosy about what they believe as they are about peanut butter.

Take for instance this guy I know who goes to a New Age doctor when he's sick, a psychic when he's confused and a synagogue on holy days. He mixes and matches beliefs the way I do candies, chips and ice cream. He's seeking happiness, but all he ends up with is a bad case of spiritual indigestion.

Unfortunately, I can't choose what my friend wants to believe any more than I can choose groceries for the person in front of me in the checkout line. If they choose to buy bologna, that's their decision.

So how can you help your searching friends? You can't make the choice for them to accept Christ, but you *can* steer them in the right direction.

THE RIGHT DIRECTION

He's the most important person in a supermarket. He knows where to find pork 'n beans. He knows where to find anchovy paste. He knows where to find everything but where you parked your car. He's the stock boy. And by following his example, you can help a searching friend find his or her way to Christ.

The apostle Peter had a bit of stock boy in him when he wrote, "Always be ready to give a defense to everyone who asks you a reason for the hope that is in you, with meekness and fear" (1 Peter 3:15, *NKJV*). In other words, always know where to send someone when they're searching for the happiness that you plainly have.

Take, for instance, this sweet lady I know named Joanne, a wife and mother with Christian roots who worships the god of outlet stores. When Joanne spots an "Everything Must Go!" sign, it triggers an adrenaline rush. Tidings of day-after-Christmas sales bring her more joy than the holiday itself. But once the sales are over and her purchases are tossed in the back of her closet, Joanne must take up the hunt for happiness once again.

I know well enough not to get between Joanne and an "Everything in the Store 50% Off!" sign. But I also know where she can find fulfillment without a credit card. She needs to know that she is someone else's costly purchase, that Christ gave His life to save hers. What Joanne needs isn't a new outfit, but a renewed relationship with Him. What I need to do as Joanne's friend is point that out to her.

SHOW THERE *IS* A DIFFERENCE BETWEEN BRANDS

Pepsi. Coke. What's the difference? To someone like myself, whose preference runs to whatever's on sale, not much. But to the rest of the world apparently there's a big one. Thanks to taste tests, we know that people can not only tell the difference in taste, but they have a favorite, too. As for me, either will do the trick when washing down a burger and fries.

Many people believe there's no difference among the world's religions, but there is. That's why it's important to get your searching friends to examine what they believe before they swallow it whole.

Danny is proud to be an American Puerto Rican. He grew up in Chicago where spirituality was a big part of his home life. Not Christianity, but spiritualism. Danny's parents practiced the sort of witchcraft we never saw on "Bewitched." It was not uncommon for Danny to come home to a séance in his living room.

If his family wasn't troubled enough, his father left when Danny was a young boy. If there was a good side to this, it was that this seemed to loosen the grip witchcraft had on Danny's mother. She decided to abandon witchcraft, and that's when bad things started happening. Danny's sister, who was in the eighth grade at the time, started getting into heavy drugs. One of his brothers joined a gang. His other brother attempted suicide.

Searching for something better, Danny and his friends were walking past Wrigley Field where an outdoor evangelism event was being held. It was there they met two on-fire teens named Awilda and Miritza, and what they said really

Smart shoppers know that not all religions are the same: Only Christianity comes with the promises that pan out.

spoke to Danny. That's when Danny began developing a relationship with the one spirit his family had not tried to contact: the Holy Spirit.

Danny got closer to Christ. He started attending the youth group at the church behind his house. There he found the strength to resist the lure of gangs and drugs. Over the years, Danny grew into a strong Christian man, never missing the spiritualism of his family's past. Danny is now a dynamic youth pastor in Chicago, where he leads other young teens to Christ.

Yes, there is a difference in what you believe, and it's far more important than where you stand on Pepsi vs. Coke. So take a shopping tip from the apostle John:

> Beloved, do not believe every spirit, but test the spirits to see whether they are from God; because many false prophets have gone out into the world (1 John 4:1).

GET THEM TO CHECK THE LABEL

If Christianity came packaged like cereal, just what would be on the nutritional label? And how would other religions measure up? While many religions offer a daily requirement of moral fiber only, Christianity comes with essential promises from a faithful God. Point these out to your searching friend.

FORTIFIED WITH PEACE, HOPE AND LOVE . . .

> Now may the Lord of peace Himself continually grant you peace in every circumstance. The Lord be with you all! (2 Thessalonians 3:16).

That being justified by His grace we might be made heirs according to the hope of eternal life (Titus 3:7).

May the Lord cause you to increase and abound in love for one another, and for all men, just as we also do for you (1 Thessalonians 3:12).

PLUS A DAILY REQUIREMENT OF FORGIVENESS . . .

If we confess our sins, He is faithful and righteous to forgive us our sins and to cleanse us from all unrighteousness (1 John 1:9).

CHRISTIANITY IS 100% GUILT FREE . . .

There is therefore now no condemnation for those who are in Christ Jesus (Romans 8:1).

WITH SATISFACTION GUARANTEED . . .

"Blessed are those who hunger and thirst for righteousness, for they shall be satisfied" (Matthew 5:6).

AND NO EXPIRATION DATE!

Jesus Christ is the same yesterday and today, yes and forever (Hebrews 13:8).

As for disappointed customers? The Bible tells us, "He who believes in Him will not be disappointed" (Romans 9:33).

GIVE THEM A FREE SAMPLE!

Learn a lesson from the sausage lady: Whether it's a treat at the end of the aisle or a taste of God's grace, no one is ever too full for a free sample—even if it's something they would never otherwise try, like a Jewish man getting a taste of Christ.

Rob is a Jewish man who grew up in New York in the late '60s. He was at Woodstock and thought himself to be open-minded about many things, except Christ. At the same time, Rob hated who he was becoming. He knew he needed "religion," but didn't know what he could believe. Judaism wasn't helping much, so Rob decided to sample other religions—Buddhism, New Age, anything but Christianity.

Then Rob moved to Hawaii, where he worked alongside a Christian lady. She was happy with her faith and Rob quickly grew tired of hearing her talk about it. One day, Rob decided to read the Bible to teach his coworker a lesson. He would read her Bible, if only to get more ammunition with which to ridicule her.

Now, the only part of the Bible that Rob owned was the Gospel of John. No sooner did Rob start reading than the Holy Spirit softened his heart and the piercing power of God's Word spoke to him. *This isn't supposed to be happening,* Rob thought. His resistance to Christ started breaking down.

Rob was especially moved by the story of the Samaritan woman at the well. When the woman said she knew the Messiah was coming, Jesus answered her, "I who speak to you am He" (John 4:26). Rob had never heard that Jesus specifically referred to Himself as the Messiah, or Christ. Before long, he realized that his resistance to Christ was based on false premises and that Jesus was in fact who He claimed to be. Soon Rob accepted Christ. He went on to Bible college and ended up a pastor.

But that's only half the story.

Rob's wife, Nora, came to know Christ through reading anti-Christian literature! A Persian Jew, Nora grew up in the Middle East and studied in Jerusalem. It was there Nora read a book containing prophecies from the Scriptures which supposedly disproved the claims of Jesus, but they instead convinced Nora that Christ was who He said He was.

Now Ron and Nora give others a "free sample" of Christ at their church in Maui.

CHECK OUT YOUR OWN SPIRITUAL EATING HABITS

Do you remember the food-group pyramid from junior high school? It's that triangle-shaped chart stacked with different food groups that makes you feel guilty about counting frosting as a side dish. Actually it's a great tool to see whether the food you are eating makes for a balanced diet. The base of the pyramid shows the food group that should comprise the bulk of your diet—cereal and grains. The middle of the pyramid contains fruits and vegetables. The next level contains meats and dairy products. The top of the pyramid contains foods you should eat sparingly, which to my chagrin are not lima beans but sweets, fats and oils.

As much as I enjoy frosting, I know that woman does not live by dessert toppings alone. If that were all I ate, I wouldn't have the muscles I need to get through the day, let alone participate in any recreational physical activity. May I be as wise in developing my spiritual eating habits.

A few years ago while in London, I got to experience something known as Speaker's Corner. Speaker's Corner is a section of Hyde Park where anyone can bring their own crate, stand on it and preach on whatever topic they want to. When I went, there were Muslims, Christians, atheists, Christian atheists (try figuring out that one) and every brand of religion between. Some of the speakers were angry. Some were loving. Some made no sense at all. Some made perfect sense. And everyone had hecklers.

The church I was attending would go to Speaker's Corner every Sunday and preach the gospel. But instead of getting on the crate myself, I would listen—not to those speaking, but to those heckling. The frightening thing was that many of the hecklers knew my Bible better than I did, including the Muslims and the atheists! So after leaving Speaker's Corner, I would spend time reading my Bible, examining the issues raised by our hecklers. Thanks to them, my faith is stronger today.

However, it shouldn't take a heckler to goad you into building spiritual muscle. Getting your daily requirement of God is at least as important as getting your daily requirement of vitamin C.

ARE YOU BUYING BOLOGNA?

Take a lesson from your butcher. Just like different meats, the Word of God can be ground up, and the truth can become diluted with unhealthy by-products known in the meat industry as filler. Make sure what you're filling up on is the real thing.

For starters, avoid the bologna. Watch out for those religions that offer only pieces of the truth. For the most part they contain unnecessary filler culled from worldly philosophies. Cults are a prime example—you never know for sure what you're biting into.

Also stay away from the daily grind. This is a favorite way of many Christians to fill up fast. For them, reading their Bibles is little more than a habit, so they get bored with what they are fed. They consume it without thinking and never end up satisfied.

But if you're asking "Where's the beef?" what you want is the real meaty stuff. You crave a true, lasting relationship with Jesus Christ.

NO SALE IS EVER FINAL

"Truly, truly, I say to you, he who hears My word, and believes Him who sent Me, has eternal life, and does not come into judgment, but has passed out of death into life."

JOHN 5:24

Few things are worse than buying something and later regretting your purchase. Take for instance that weird juice flavor that nature never intended. No, not apricot-kiwi or strawberry-banana, but Clamato, a mixture of clam and tomato. Blecch!

That stuff sounds too weird for even my stomach to digest. But if I bought it and didn't like it, most stores would be kind enough to take it back. Or I could just call up the number on the label for a refund.

Buying into bad beliefs can be a bad experience, too. They will invariably leave you unsatisfied and empty. Fortunately, it's not too late to exchange them for Christ. So if a friend has the spiritual munchies, lead her down the right aisle. Inform her about the difference between brands and get her to check the label. And never put your bread in the bottom of a bag.

That last one has nothing to do with how to shop for religion. It's just another important grocery tip my mother taught me.

GROCERY CHECKLIST

- What's the biggest difference between Christianity and the "brand of faith" your friend is considering?

- What other things are they filling up on besides God?

- What is one way you can give them a tasty sample of Christianity?

- How can you improve your own spiritual eating habits?

Free Inside Specially Marked Packages

Working in advertising, I have learned all kinds of cool but trivial stuff. Like how they get the right championship team on the front of the cereal box within hours of the Super Bowl postgame show.

Several days prior to the big game, a cereal company actually prints up two sets of Super Bowl theme boxes, each featuring a possible winning team. Each box has a picture of one of the two teams and a banner that says something like "Congratulations Super Bowl XXXVII Champions." These two sets of boxes remain empty and unfolded until the night of the game. Better known as box flats, the unassembled packages are loaded into the back of two semitrailer trucks like semiprecious cargo. The trucks then head to the plant where the cereal is produced and packaged. Once there, these secured trucks are backed up and parked against a wall, so no one can get to the box flats inside.

Meanwhile, an executive representing the cereal company does his difficult part to ensure the success of this important production: He attends the Super Bowl game. After the halftime extravaganza, blimps, overblown commercial spots and the incidental final score, the executive picks up a phone and calls the cereal plant, authorizing them to fill the correct champion boxes and destroy the winners that never were. All of that to sell a bowl of cereal.

THE INSIDE SCOOP

Let's get real. As cool and colorful as the outside of a cereal box can be, what we really want to know is what's free inside. I'm not talking about an extra scoop of raisins, but the various prizes found rustling in cellophane near the bottom. Plastic submarines you fill with baking soda. Rubber band-propelled cars. Pens with disappearing ink. Stuff you won't find in any store, but only inside specially marked packages.

As a kid, I knew those free prizes were cooler than the cereal. I would eat frosted tree bark if it came with the right toy. Every week I would dig to the bottom of a new box as if searching for gold. My dad, on the other hand, would request cereals with no prizes, which were also the cereals with no taste. Unless of course, there was a cereal with an offer for free golf balls.

As a beginning copywriter, I cut my teeth writing commercials for those free prizes—glow-in-the-dark stickers, iron-on patches, candy samples, instant-winner game pieces and my all-time favorite, the multipurpose musical sticker dispenser. It made music. It was filled with stickers. Why you would want or need both at the same time, only a hyperactive seven-year-old would know.

THERE'S A FREE PRIZE INSIDE EVERY CHRISTIAN, TOO!

For the wages of sin is death, but the free gift of God is eternal life in Christ Jesus our Lord.

ROMANS 6:23

Cereal companies get credit for coming up with the concept of free prizes, but that's not where it started. The original free prize inside was a gift from God. No, not that little glass of grape juice you get during Sunday services but the free gift of salvation— and the Holy Spirit as an added bonus! But if you think you have to wait until you're dead to enjoy this gift, you're in for a surprise. God's gift includes more than a lifetime pass to heaven; you also get goodies like love, joy, peace, patience, kindness, goodness, faithfulness, gentleness and self-control (see Galatians 5:22,23). Try finding those in a box of Cocoa Puffs! And just like a free prize in your favorite cereal, these gifts are yours to enjoy as soon as you can rip into them.

FRUIT CHEWS

Weird as it sounds, finding a good chewer is difficult. True, people you see in commercials are professional actors, but finding one who can chew convincingly on camera is tough. It's not uncommon for us to look at 50 child actors to find one who can say "Mmm-m-m" and mean it.

A convincing "Mmm-m-m" consists of more than an oversized bite of cereal (which, if you watch carefully, might not even be chewed). A good "Mmm-m-m" is usually followed by raised eyebrow action and a nod to Mom. Try doing that the next time you eat dinner at home; it's even harder with a camera pointed at you and a dozen or so crew members standing around waiting for you to get it right. Eating professionally is tough stuff.

On the other hand, finding someone who looks happy opening a free prize is easy. They don't even have to act. But finding a Christian who enjoys the gifts of God can be just as tough as finding a good chewer. Nothing is more embarrassing than trying to share Christ with someone who never smiles, only to find out that person has been saved for 20 years!

Enjoying your free gifts from God should be as easy as enjoying free prizes in your cereal. These gifts are not good china to be dusted off and used only when your pastor comes over for dinner. The fruits of the Holy Spirit are to be enjoyed every day.

SPECIALLY MARKED PACKAGES

I once had a friend who owned a beagle named Lilly. Lilly was your typical beagle except for one minor canine quirk: She didn't limit her eating to Alpo. One night Lilly's stomach was bloating, so we rushed her to the animal hospital. The veterinarian took an X-ray to determine what the problem might be. Inside Lilly's stomach they found staples, paper clips and a few coins. No one ever guessed all those items were inside the indiscriminating beagle.

Does it take an X-ray for others to know that Christ is inside you? A free prize won't convince anyone to buy cereal if no one knows the free prize is inside the box. That's why the packages are specially marked! Good and faithful servant, don't keep your gifts safely tucked away inside (see Matthew 25:14-30). Take off the wrapping and use them today!

PAID IN FULL

Waiting until you get to heaven to enjoy your faith is like the man who saved his money to buy a ticket for an ocean cruise. So that he could comfortably afford his passage, the man decided he would eat nothing but saltine crackers during the voyage. While others would go to the ship's dining room to eat breakfast, this man would eat crackers. While other guests enjoyed a delicious lunch, this man solemnly ate his saltines.

One evening, while everyone else on the ship dined on fabulous cuisine, this man stood at the railing on deck and quietly ate his crackers. A curious deckhand came up to the man and said, "Sir, for this entire journey, I have only seen you eat crackers. Why haven't you enjoyed the meals in the dining room?"

The man replied, "After paying so much for the ticket, I did not want to spend any more on elaborate meals."

The deckhand said to him, "Why, sir, this is a cruise! All your meals are free!"

Your ticket to heaven comes with more free perks than just a midnight buffet and ice sculptures. Don't keep them under wraps. Enjoy them now.

YOU'RE IN GOOD HANDS

When you pass through the waters, I will be with you; and through the rivers, they will not overflow you. When you walk through the fire, you will not be scorched, nor will the flame burn you. For I am the LORD your God . . . your Savior.

ISAIAH 43:2,3

And we know that God causes all things to work together for good to those who love God, to those who are called according to His purpose.

ROMANS 8:28

We all know from Sunday School that faith in God is the ultimate flood, fire and disaster insurance as described in Isaiah 43, but did you know that the Bible also gives you assurance that God has your best interests in mind?

Nobody knows that better than Addie and Harry. Addie, a young kindergarten teacher and devoted Christian, met Harry at her local church. They fell in love and started dating seriously.

Harry then went off to Bible college, so their relationship continued by mail. Soon after Harry left for college, God put a call on Addie's life to go to the mission field—not just anywhere, but to Africa. As much as Addie loved Harry, she also knew God's will must come first. So Addie wrote Harry a letter explaining how she was going to follow God's will for her life.

Meanwhile, God had also spoken to Harry about the direction of his life. God had put the mission field on Harry's heart as well. Not just anywhere, but Africa. Harry knew he had to be obedient to God. And as much as Harry loved Addie and wanted to marry her, he wrote to Addie about how he had to put God's will first and follow His call to Africa.

Well, Harry and Addie's letters crossed in the mail.

That was more than 50 years ago. Since then, my Aunt Addie and Uncle Harry have worked in the mission field in

Africa and other places. Everywhere they go, they openly enjoy their faith, and their story has

Think you need to have your life together to enjoy Chist? The Lord is the very help you need when you're going to pieces. "God is our refuge and strength, a very present help in trouble" (Psalm 46:1).

been a tremendous blessing to others. Harry and Addie had the assurance that if they did God's will, God would do what was best for them.

A LIFETIME SUPPLY—AND THEN SOME

He who sows righteousness gets a true reward.
PROVERBS 11:18

Imagine getting so much of Christ that your life overflows with His joy until the day you die—and beyond. That's exactly what happened to Pastor Jack. Pastor Jack and his wife, Kathy, started out as missionaries in Korea, where they founded an orphanage for young boys left homeless by the Korean War. Over the years, the orphanage grew and so did the numbers of loving parents around the world who opened their homes to these boys, thanks to this American couple.

After 30 years of working in the orphanage in Korea, Pastor Jack and Kathy returned home to Chicago. But Jack did not retire. Instead, his love kept on blossoming as he took on other pastoral duties. Unfortunately, Pastor Jack's health started deteriorating. A lump was found in his lung that would not respond to treatment, and Pastor Jack grew weaker, spending less time behind the pulpit and more time in bed.

Finally, the day came when the Lord called Jack home. Though Pastor Jack's passing was quiet and uneventful, his funeral arrangements were delayed for several days. Why? Because orphans from around the world who had grown up to be fathers, strong Christians, doctors and businessmen all wanted to attend Pastor Jack's service. So, about a week after his death, a service was held celebrating his life and arrival in heaven. The service was SRO—standing room only! People from all corners of the globe continued to share in the joy that Pastor Jack had received and given freely.

YOU'LL FIND FREE COURAGE, TOO

For God has not given us a spirit of fear, but of power
and of love and of a sound mind.
2 TIMOTHY 1:7, NKJV

Faith not only gives you the ability to move mountains, but the courage to storm a mountain on horseback as well. I am referring to the time I foolishly decided to see Scotland by horse. You should know that horseback riding is an area where my skill level and experience rank right up there with my ability to perform brain surgery.

I had signed on for what looked to be a quaint trail-riding excursion in Argyll, Scotland, having read about it in a travel brochure. Trail riding sounded easy enough, maybe a step above pony rides at the carnival. Little did I know that in the Highlands, trail riding is anything but a walk in the park—more like kamikaze steeplechasing! When I showed up in Scotland, I was startled to find that my riding companions consisted of seven French equestrian ninjas. However, Scotland was beautiful and my deposit was nonrefundable, so I was determined to stick it out for the week. But if I was to come back alive, I would desperately need the courage that comes with faith in God.

Seeing my lack of experience, our trail guide assigned me to ride Monte, a horse so gentle and trusted that this horse was used with children in the Special Olympics. Our guide took pride in the fact that no one had ever fallen off Monte. Well, if that was true, I made Scottish history twice that week.

We were up in the hills, jumping over fences and racing

through the woods when Monte started to quicken his gallop. Before I knew what was happening, I had fallen off. And the only thing scarier than falling off a galloping horse is getting back on.

I was terrified. I started praying to God, not only for courage, but that Monte would feel the love and peace of his Creator through me. Again I fell off and this time the hooves of seven other horses galloped past my head. Again I summoned the courage to get back on.

Though it is unlikely I will ever get on a horse again—not even at a carnival—this adventure gave me the chance to unwrap the courage God had tucked inside me.

COLLECT ALL FOUR!

Ever notice how there's rarely just one prize offered on a box of cereal? The prize may come in a series of colors, or there will be four different character figurines with a headline shouting "Collect 'Em! Trade 'Em!" (Throw 'em away!) By the time you've collected all four, you've bought more cereal than you could eat in three lifetimes.

But with Christianity, you get all the promises and all the gifts all at once—just by asking! Check out what you get with the fruit of the Spirit:

> But the fruit of the Spirit is love, joy, peace, patience, kindness, goodness, faithfulness, gentleness, self-control (Galatians 5:22,23).

And if your collection isn't complete, don't bother with a self-addressed stamped envelope. All you need to do is ask:

> "And all things you ask in prayer, believing, you shall receive" (Matthew 21:22).

WHERE THERE'S NO PRIZE, THERE'S JUST FLAKES

Cereal boxes, like books and cars, are one of those things where what you see on the outside is sometimes better than what's inside. We've all purchased our share of boxes with a champion on the front, only to wind up with a losing taste.

But if the package isn't pleasing, if there's no prize waiting to be found, no one is going to care what's inside. So make your life a reflection of the Life that's within. Unwrap the free gifts that God has given you. Because if you don't openly enjoy your faith, no one else will.

Chapter 11

New and Improved Christians

Ever buy something that claims to be "new and improved," only to be confused as to what's so new and improved about it?

This happened with a cereal account I worked on. A well-known brand that had been around awhile was eager to generate some product news to boost sales. One of the ways to do this is to improve the taste of the cereal. Now, a taste improvement doesn't have to mean a drastic change; just enough to validate the coveted "Even More Taste!" banner on the front of the box.

The taste of the product can be improved in any number of ways—sweeter marshmallows, crunchier O's, bigger flakes. Even a change in color can influence your perception of taste. But in this case we had a real problem. Because the cereal had always been made from 100% whole wheat, we couldn't figure out how to describe "even more taste." Could flakes made from 100% whole wheat be fortified with 120% whole-wheat taste?

That's when we decided to enlist the help of regular people. Taste tests were held to find out what ordinary consumers would say about the new taste. Was it bigger? Better? Browner? Well, after spending a week watching people chew, we were no closer to an answer. Worse, one test group didn't even like the new taste, while the other group failed to notice *anything* new about the taste.

Product improvements often get a lot of attention for the fraction of a difference they make in the product's performance. Consider the "revolutionary" Mach 3 razor from Gillette. This new razor has three blades instead of two, giving its users an extra, extra, extra close shave. Millions of dollars went into product development, research, packaging, advertising and in-store displays, all for the sake of an almost imperceptible reduction in the length of a man's whiskers. But for the millions of men who willingly take a blade (or two or three) to their faces every day, that fraction of a whisker length makes all the difference in the world when choosing a razor.

THE ULTIMATE IMPROVEMENT

Then there are my personal new and improved favorites: reduced-fat potato chips, Double Stuff Oreos and better tasting Metamucil. Oh yes, and clump-free kitty litter. But if you think Double Stuff Oreos are as good as it gets, check out the ultimate product improvement as described in Paul's letter to the Church at Corinth:

> Therefore if any man is in Christ, he is a new creature; the old things passed away; behold, new things have come (2 Corinthians 5:17).

Paul tells us that as Christians we are new creatures, and for those of us who have made our share of mistakes, that's great news! We get a clean slate, a new taste of God, a brand-new outlook on life. But just how does that translate to the way we live? Are we just bigger, browner flakes, or are there perceptible improvements?

Like any new and improved product, being a new creature in Christ means a lot of little changes that will add up to make a big difference. One of those improvements is added strength:

> Yet those who wait for the LORD will gain new strength; they will mount up with wings like eagles, they will run and not get tired, they will walk and not become weary (Isaiah 40:31).

Back in April 1995, I was behind a two-way mirror in Miami, Florida, working on a product improvement for yogurt. Not a new taste, not a less lumpy texture, but yogurt enriched with the benefits of fiber. (Hey, anything's possible.) I was listening to women talk about their impressions of this yogurt when I received a phone call from my oldest sister, telling me my father's health had just taken a turn for the worse.

At the time, my father was in the hospital, suffering complications from a kidney disease. Needless to say, my father meant more to me than fiber in yogurt. So, with my supervisor's approval, I abandoned the test groups and headed for the airport. Unfortunately, I missed the only direct flight to Grand Rapids, Michigan. So I got on the next possible flight, a plane that broke down in North Carolina, where I was transferred to another plane that was again delayed. I finally showed up in Grand Rapids six hours after I was supposed to arrive.

When I got to the hospital, my mother was pacing the lobby, hysterical, not only because my father had already passed away, but because she feared something had happened to me, too. My sisters were gathered around my deceased father in a cold, empty room, not wanting to move his body until I could be there. It was awful, awful, awful.

Losing a parent, no matter how prepared you think you are, is a terrible experience. But my faith in Christ gave me the strength to get through it. For starters, I knew my dad had gone to heaven. I also took comfort in knowing that God wouldn't put me through anything I couldn't endure. This knowledge didn't take the pain out of losing my father, but it did help me deal with it.

LOST AND FOUND

Becoming a Christian doesn't mean you will enjoy a problem-free life, but God does promise to give you what you will need to deal with the inevitable difficulties of living in a fallen world. Like getting fired—a common enough experience, but an inescapable fact of life when you work in advertising.

I remember the day it happened to me. We had just finished work on a provocative advertising campaign for a local hospital. We liked the campaign a lot, but it made the hospital a bit, uh, nervous. Actually, it caused the hospital so much discomfort that they fired our agency. And when a client fires an agency, an irreversible chain reaction begins. My boss was called into his boss's office, and before long everyone was whispering, "Did you hear who was let go?" But my boss wasn't the only one on the hit list. By the end of the day, eight people would lose their jobs.

Still, I wasn't too caught up in the drama of who was on the firing line, because I was caught up in my own dilemma—I had lost my wallet. I remember thinking how losing a wallet was worse than losing a job, because I would have to go through the hassle of getting new identification, canceling my credit cards and living in fear that someone could be using my Visa to charge thousands of dollars' worth of pizza at Chuck E. Cheese's.

After an emergency cab ride home to find my wallet safe on my kitchen counter, I returned to work only to have a member of personnel tell me that I had been let go. All in all, I took it in good stride, mostly because I knew God had a plan for my life. Besides, I wouldn't have to replace my driver's license.

A NEW OUTLOOK

Be renewed in the spirit of your mind, and put on the new self, which in the likeness of God has been created in righteousness and holiness of the truth.

EPHESIANS 4:23,24

Product improvements go hand in hand with product claims of being "new," like ads trumpeting new flavors of Hamburger Helper. Three Cheese Macaroni is not exactly earth shattering, but it's just different enough to add a little spice to your daily grind.

A lady who used to attend my church is a good example of Three Cheese Macaroni. Joy* was quite the optimist; God gave her a smile and she was bound and determined to use it. Before I was fired, Joy noticed that I had been complaining about my work. I complained about the clients, I complained about my hours, I complained about other employees' complaining. Joy would listen to me complain and never complain in kind. Instead, she would offer me a smile and a prayer.

After one particularly tough week, Joy gave me a little toy teddy bear to cheer me up. Well, her gesture not only touched me, it embarrassed me, because Joy, the lady with the ear-to-ear smile, was a single mother trying desperately to find a steady job. She would gladly have taken anything without complaint, whether it meant working nights or nine to five. Those past few

* Not her real name, but it definitely suited her.

weeks had been especially painful for Joy, as her brother had been recently murdered.

So between the two of us, who had the renewed spirit? Who should have been comforting whom? A renewed spirit not only could have helped me to deal with my daily grind, but would have helped me to comfort the one who *really* needed it.

NEW THINKING FOR ROUGH WATERS

And do not be conformed to this world, but be transformed by the renewing of your mind, that you may prove what is that good and acceptable and perfect will of God.
ROMANS 12:2, *NKJV*

A few years ago, I had the unique experience of taking a group of urban teens camping in Wisconsin. Since their idea of fresh air was exhaust fumes from a new bus, I was certain this trip would prove to be a transforming experience for them.

Our adventure began with a canoe trip downriver—not in little two-man canoes but a mass-transit version large enough to carry our entire group. Close to 20 of us piled into that canoe. Like city mice in the country, we had no idea what we were doing. Within seconds of splashing off, we had rammed our canoe into a big rock, puncturing the fiberglass bottom and leaving a gash about two inches wide. As water started to seep into the canoe, the teens started to panic. But one of them had an idea that only a teen could have come up with. Why not repair the hole with bubble gum? Since bubble gum is never in short supply when teens are around, this thinking probably saved all our necks.

Everyone started unwrapping bubble gum and chewing frantically. There was super-sour grape, super bubble, the classic pink, even the stuff that squirts in the middle. And little by little, colorful piece by colorful piece, the teens patched up the hole. It was all we needed to get safely to the campgrounds, where the canoe could be more permanently repaired.

This was the first of many events during the week that required our group to think differently—the next would be dealing with outdoor plumbing. God loosened the grip of many city influences that week to touch the hearts of these teens.

CANNING THE "CANNOTS"

Create in me a clean heart, O God, and renew
a steadfast spirit within me.
PSALM 51:10

Many times newness simply means a new attitude, like in the case of Ball Jars. This long-established brand posed an interesting problem. In the days before Frigidaires, microwave ovens and take-out Chinese, canning was an integral part of life and the fortunes of the Ball family had risen with the popularity of their jars. But in recent years, few women have been willing to invest time or energy in canning because they saw it as needless work in the age of convenience.

So the job in promoting Ball Jars wasn't just to change the advertising, but to create advertising that would change an attitude. The goal was to get the audience to perceive canning as a fun activity—so much fun they wouldn't mind making a mess or cleaning it up.

The new theme line was "When's the last time you had a ball in your kitchen?" Instead of showing grandma slaving over a hot stove, the ads featured young women licking as much fresh jam off their fingers as they put into Ball Jars. It worked. The new attitude created new interest in canning.

In the same way, renewed strength in Christ can change your attitude about "old things" or old problems you don't want to face. And you will come to realize that with Christ, you *can* do anything (see Philippians 4:13).

What's in a name? Remember when KFC used to be Kentucky Fried Chicken and Coca-Cola Classic was just plain Coke? Companies change product names for a multitude of reasons, but there is one name that hasn't changed and never will—"the name which is above every name" (Philippians 2:9).

FROM SILLY PUTTY TO POTTER'S CLAY

I went down to the potter's house, and there he was, making something at the wheel. And the vessel that he made of clay was marred in the hand of the potter; so he made it again into another vessel, as it seemed good to the potter to make. . . . "Can I not do with you as this potter?" says the LORD. "Look, as the clay is in the potter's hand, so are you in My hand."
JEREMIAH 18:3-6, NKJV

Silly Putty is one of the few products you simply cannot improve. After nearly half a century, Silly Putty still comes in an egg in that same funky color and you can still stretch it, bounce it, snap it and copy your favorite comic strip characters with it.

On the other hand, you and I are like the potter's clay described in the book of Jeremiah; we are always being reshaped, remodeled and improved. When I'm not at my best, when holiness seems so far removed from my life it couldn't be seen by the Hubble Telescope, it's nice to know that God isn't done with me yet; that He's always working to mold me into someone better and that He won't stop until the work is completed:

He who has begun a good work in you will complete it until the day of Jesus Christ (Philippians 1:6, *NKJV*).

Take for instance this teen I know with a *tat*. What's a tat? A tat is what you end up with when you decide halfway through the tattooing process that you don't want a tattoo. And the only thing that looks worse than a tattoo is half a tattoo. This teen, who was just trying to be different like everyone else, started to get a vine tattooed around his upper arm. Somewhere between his triceps and biceps, he realized this wasn't such a cool idea. Now he sports a permanent reminder of his mistake. But it's nice to know that in God's eyes our tats and mistakes can be undone, our hearts remodeled and reworked. We are never too hopeless or too far gone that God would give up on us.

AS GOOD AS IT GETS

With all the product improvements out there, the one thing we cannot improve upon is God's plan for salvation. And who would want to? Our acceptance of Jesus Christ as Lord and Savior allows us to spend eternity with Him in heaven. We are also given an open line of communication with our Creator, and we receive a number of useful gifts unwrapped and ready to use. All this and a loving Lord who is the same yesterday, today and tomorrow. It doesn't get any better than that!

So if someone you know is looking for a new and improved way of life, tell them to try the one faith that cannot be improved—faith in an unchanging Lord.

PART III

FREE INSPIRATIONAL STUFF!

Chapter 12

The Man Who Walks on Water vs. the Man Who Flies

The summer of '96 I took a leave of absence from advertising to work with teens in Europe. There I experienced some incredible evangelistic opportunities in places the typical tourist never sees. One of these places was known as the "British Bronx." These were British Council Flats located about 40 miles outside London—not too dissimilar from our own government housing projects. They were filled with single moms, junkies and others who desperately needed the love of Christ.

At the last minute, I was asked to share at an outdoor outreach there and I was anything but prepared. To make matters worse, it was particularly hot and the audience was mostly heckling teens who were not too shy to tell us how they felt about Christians evangelizing with megaphones. Now, if this had actually been the Bronx, the crowd might have pulled semiautomatic weapons from under their jackets. But as this was England, they threw eggs—farm-fresh ammunition which they freely launched at those of us speaking.

My feet were sizzling in the summer heat and I didn't feel like cleaning omelet off my sandals. What could I say to keep this young crowd from throwing eggs at me? What experience could I share to tune them in? So instead of diving right in about the man who walks on water, I started talking about the man who flies: Michael Jordan.

I told them how I had met the basketball superstar and had the opportunity to work with him on a few occasions. But even more impressive than Michael Jordan, I went on to tell them, were the inner-city teens I had met who had the courage to follow Christ.

It worked.

They put their eggs down and tuned in to the message. My shoes, among other things, were saved.

AIR JORDAN

Working in advertising includes bigger perks than just free cereal and fabric softener. Like meeting a lot of celebrities and athletes, including Michael Jordan. I would be dishonest if I said it wasn't exciting meeting him or that his autographed basketball hasn't come in handy at a youth meeting.

The first time I met Michael Jordan was during the filming of a national television commercial. The lighting crew and advertising agency had arrived early to go through last-minute details. A few dozen people were milling about when, all of a sudden, someone whispered, "He's here!" And no, they weren't referring to my boss.

The entire chemistry of the room changed the moment Michael Jordan walked in. It was as if the air were electrified. A hush fell over the crowd and all eyes turned to him. I hadn't been so excited since being a kid on Christmas morning!

But Michael didn't wait for us to roll out the red carpet and treat him like someone special. Instead, Michael took the initiative to shake *our* hands. "Ginger, it's a pleasure to meet you," he said.

Wow! Talk about the ultimate greeter for church. Michael Jordan, the superstar of all superstars, went out of his way to make *me* feel special.

MAJOR FANS IN GALILEE

If only it were as easy to get people excited about Christ as they are about today's sports stars. I don't know about you, but I've never had to buy a front-center pew seat from a scalper, no matter how famous or exciting the speaker. But that's not the way it always was.

Two millennia ago in rural Galilee, Jesus drew big crowds without the help of a public relations firm or mass media. Once a crowd of 5,000 showed up with no reserved seating or concession stands. Yet no one went hungry; Christ fed them. Can you imagine going to a baseball game today where the vendors pass out free hot dogs, peanuts and Cracker Jack until everyone is full?

Wherever He put in a personal appearance, Jesus did more than lead His team

Standing Room Only!
"And Jesus, when He came out, saw a great multitude and was moved with compassion for them" (Mark 6:34, NKJV).

to victory: Christ taught what it takes to be victorious. He demonstrated the kind of discipline it takes to resist every kind of temptation. He showed the courage to stand up to what was wrong and the strength to do what was right, yet He had the humility to serve instead of expecting to be served. Jesus Christ was a true champion and that's why His fan club is still growing today.

FROM CHAMPION TO CHERUBS

Somehow through the centuries though, that champion portrait of Christ has been replaced with the picture of a Man who hangs out with sheep. You know what I'm talking about: those stained-glass windows and velvet paintings of the Good Shepherd with chubby cherubs floating around His head. Don't get me wrong, they're beautiful; I enjoy them as much as the next person. But with our artistic and cultural emphasis on the gentleness of the Lord, His champion status has become, well, sort of lost. Why do we rarely portray Jesus as the One who stood up to the powerful Pharisees?

Imagine for a moment a heavyweight boxer surrounded by chubby cherubs. All of a sudden, his biceps don't seem to bulge as impressively. Maybe it's time to present a picture of Christ that speaks to the world where it lives—a portrait of a champion like you would expect to see on a cereal box instead of a church window. Let's not fashion it out of stained glass, however, but with our lives.

I WANT TO BE LIKE ~~MIKE~~ CHRIST

Be imitators of me, just as I also am of Christ.
1 CORINTHIANS 11:1

Advertisers know the importance of role models, from Tony the Tiger to Tiger Woods. Some of them are winners, some are losers. Some are chumps, some are champions. Still, people want to dress like them, eat like them, play like them, smell like them. People really want to be like Mike.

I know this from bringing a Michael Jordan-autographed basketball to my youth group. Since I'm probably the only person in Chicago who is not a basketball fan, I am certain this basketball was a gift from God. He knew how useful it would be in youth meetings. Never had I held teens' attention like the night I brought the ball. One Michael Jordan fanatic, Eddie, was particularly enthralled. Now, Eddie wasn't a bad kid; in fact, he really loved the Lord. But at the time, Eddie was into Michael—*really* into Michael. Not only did he wear his #23 jersey everywhere, Eddie would carry around his Michael Jordan scrapbook and video collection, which he would watch before and after youth meetings. And when it came time for prayer requests, somewhere between praying for help on his biology test and praying for his parents, Eddie prayed that he would meet his idol.

Tired of playing second string to Michael Jordan, not to mention seeing the same red jersey every week, I got Eddie's attention with the ball then challenged him with a few questions. "Eddie, what can this autographed ball do for you? Can it do more for you than a Bible?" Eddie didn't know what to say.

We began talking about super athletes and what it meant to be like Mike vs. being like Christ. Idolizing a great athlete and embracing his training regimen might help you win a big game, but you'll lose the big picture. We talked about the characteristics of a champion that Jesus displayed and the potential for champion-caliber character inside of Eddie. It was an excellent opportunity to get Eddie to examine just whom he was worshiping. Now Eddie is over Michael Jordan and into girls.

IT'S NOT THE SHOES

"For to everyone who has shall more be given, and he shall
have an abundance; but from the one who does not have, even
what he does have shall be taken away."

MATTHEW 25:29

The night I talked with Eddie at youth group, I learned something important, too. Eddie pointed out to me that a person is a champion not just because of his talent, but because he does something with it. He makes the most of the gifts God gave him instead of making excuses why he doesn't.

Nicoli is a prime example. After I left England, I traveled to Bulgaria where I had the privilege of staying with various local families. One family I stayed with had a son in America who at that very time was competing in the Summer Olympics in Atlanta. His name was Nicoli and he was representing Bulgaria in a sport that is not a high-coverage event, that being the two-man crew team. There would be no shoe named after him, no commercials for soft drinks. Just a chance to do his best.

I thought of all the hours and hours Nicoli had practiced to compete in this low-profile Olympic event. He had gotten out of bed early every day for years, devoting his life for this one chance to compete against the best in the world. Since Nicoli was in Atlanta, I got to sleep in his bedroom, where he displayed his many medals, ribbons and trophies. This got me thinking: *If God had a trophy case displaying the fruits of my efforts, would it be full or empty? What am I doing with the talent God has given me?*

After the Games were ended, Nicoli decided to extend his visa and stay in America awhile longer. Call it coincidence or call it God's working, but he would be staying just miles from one of my sisters in Detroit, Michigan. So Nicoli's mother asked me to bring a bag of his belongings back to America for her son, including a pair of athletic shoes. I gladly said yes, wanting very much to meet their son.

I also secretly wanted to try on Nicoli's shoes. After all, how often do you get a chance to stand in the shoes of an Olympic athlete? Not that I really thought they would give me instant strength or motivation, but if Nicoli's shoes were in any way responsible for his success, I was going to run right out and buy me a pair. So I slipped on the shoes and . . . nothing.

Nicoli's success had nothing to do with his shoes, in spite of their brand name. He was a champion for the same reason any other champion is: He made the most of the ability God had given him.

WHAT DOES IT TAKE TO BE A CHAMPION?

According to the folks at Wheaties, the Breakfast of Champions, it takes more than athletic ability to be a champion. One must exhibit the characteristics of a champion off the playing field as well. That's why this cereal has had only a handful of official champions over the past 50 years.

According to the Bible, there are high standards for being a champion for Christ, too. For starters, you never quit:

> Therefore, since we have so great a cloud of witnesses surrounding us, let us also lay aside every encumbrance, and the sin which so easily entangles us, and let us run with endurance the race that is set before us, fixing our eyes on Jesus (Hebrews 12:1,2).

Do you want to be a champion for the Lord? Then you will need to put as much dedication and effort into your faith as a champion athlete puts into his sport. Here are six characteristics of a champion that separate a great athlete from a benchwarmer. Remember these and you'll never ride the pines again:

A CHAMPION IS WELL TRAINED

Be diligent to present yourself approved to God, a worker who does not need to be ashamed, rightly dividing the word of truth (2 Timothy 2:15, *NKJV*).

YOU MUST BE FAST ON YOUR FEET

Now flee from youthful lusts, and pursue righteousness, faith, love and peace, with those who call on the Lord from a pure heart (2 Timothy 2:22).

BE A TEAM PLAYER

Therefore encourage one another, and build up one another, just as you also are doing (1 Thessalonians 5:11).

AIM HIGH

Set your mind on the things above, not on the things that are on earth (Colossians 3:2).

KEEP A WINNING ATTITUDE

Thanks be to God, who gives us the victory through our Lord Jesus Christ (1 Corinthians 15:57).

**REMEMBER, YOU'RE WORTH MORE THAN ANY
MULTIMILLION-DOLLAR CONTRACT**

You have been bought with a price: therefore glorify God
in your body (1 Corinthians 6:20).

Champion Today, History Tomorrow

Remember Gertrude Ederle? For those of you who remember
her, you probably feel very old all of a sudden. For those of you
who went "Huh?" you'll feel the same way someday when some
kid doesn't recognize Michael Jordan.

Gertrude Ederle was the first woman to swim across the
English Channel, which she did in August of 1926. Since then
many have achieved this feat, and like many other sports heroes,
Gertrude has been all but forgotten. That's why it's important to
focus on the one timeless champion, Jesus Christ. If you're going
to strive to be like anyone, pattern your life after the One who
will be around longer than just a few seasons:

And He is the image of the invisible God, the first-born
of all creation (Colossians 1:15).

Dare to Be a Champion

Face it. The thrill of walking on water only comes to those who
are willing to get their feet wet. I learned this from another
Bulgarian teenager, a girl named Bojidara, who was better
known as Dare.

Hers was a nickname suited to her courage. She was from
Sophia, the capital of a country that redefines poverty. Like most

Bulgarians, Dare had little money and few possessions. But God had given Dare a gift, a talent. She could play the violin. Really play. Everywhere she went, Dare took her violin and practiced several hours each day. In the mountains, in small villages, in places I never knew existed.

By the age of 14, Dare was playing her violin in orchestras throughout Europe. And Dare wasn't playing second fiddle, either; she was the star soloist. But concert halls weren't the only places Dare played. She would play on street corners, too. She didn't do this so much for the money as she did to help her deal with rejection. Dare would continue to play her violin regardless of whether passersby stopped to give her praise.

When she was 17, Dare was offered scholarships to some of the most prestigious music schools in the United States, which

It's gotta be the shoes, right? Wrong.

she declined. I was shocked, thinking someone from a country with so little would jump at the chance to study in a country with so much. But Dare knew that the only place to study European music was in, uh, Europe. Primarily, Vienna. So she dared to go to Vienna without a job, a scholarship or knowledge of the German language. Dare trusted God to provide for her, and He did.

Dare found a job, a place to stay and time to study German as well as practice. She worked her way through music school, making the most of the talent God gave her.

Now, I play the tuba. And to be quite honest, I don't think I have talent. The last time I played was for a variety show in high school, only to have a pie thrown in my face. But I have since discovered the talents and abilities God gave me. And just like Dare or a super athlete, it's up to me to make the most of these gifts. Dare taught me a lot about music, but more importantly I learned from her to have the courage to be my best.

WHO WANTS TO MEET WHOM?

We all know what the reaction would be if a champion like Michael Jordan walked into the room. But would the reaction be the same if that champion were Jesus Christ?

Come to think of it, Christ *does* walk into a room every time you do. So make sure you're not just watching a champion but being one. After all, life is not a spectator sport. And you don't have to be Michael Jordan to be a champion. You don't even have to be the guy who drives the Zamboni. All you have to do is to make the most of what God gave you so that somewhere, sometime, a youth leader might save his sandals by mentioning *your* name. Hey, stranger things have happened.

As Not Seen on TV

Indeed, the very hairs on your head are all numbered. Do not fear;
you are of more value than many sparrows.

LUKE 12:7

Ever wonder why you can never seem to get your hair (let alone your tuna casserole) to look as perfect as in TV commercials? You should know it can take a team of people *weeks* to make a model's hair look perfect and frizz-free. But as Christians, it's comforting to know that we aren't supposed to be perfect. God made us to be irregular humans with bodies perfectly designed for doing what He wants each of us to do. And only a handful of us were called to be supermodels.

I myself have had many bad-hair days, but the last one was a real doozy. In my neverending quest for the perfect hair color (which is, of course, anything *but* the color God blessed me with at birth), I went to a beauty salon to become an *ash blonde*. This was a newfangled color I had seen in a commercial featuring cool music and models with perfect bodies and hair. Of course, results may vary, and my hair didn't end up looking anything like what I had seen on TV. On my head, ash blonde resembled more of a weird soot brown. In fact, the color was so bad it even horrified the beautician, who attempted to color my hair again, free of charge.

Major mistake.

This time, I ended up with a toxic shade of orange.

With my pride now damaged as well as my hair, I called in sick to work the next day in order to make an appointment with yet another colorist. Now, this hair colorist worked at an expensive, trendy salon where everyone wore black and had names like Fabio and Dominic. But even she couldn't salvage my hair. Once again my hair turned a color that nature and Clairol never intended.

But that wasn't my first bad-hair experience. There was the time I went to summer camp as a counselor. I was going for the natural look, but since the camp was in the humid air of the Missouri Ozarks, the natural look meant natural disaster. My hair was so frizzy, a little girl came up to me and yanked it, thinking it was a clown wig.

Then there was the Bad Home Perm of '79. The only thing worse than the smell of the perm was the look of it. I looked like Greg Brady during his ill-conceived "groovy" stage. All photos recording the aftermath of this disaster have since been destroyed.

But while I can now laugh at most of my bad-hair experiences, one is still a painful memory. This was the haircut in eighth grade when I was trying to look like a model instead of like me. As a 13-year-old girl despairing of ever seeing the other side of puberty, I would page through teen fashion magazines and dream of looking like a cover girl. I remember one model in particular who caught my eye. She was French with big green eyes and really short, cropped, light-brown hair. I wanted that hair.

Fashion wasn't the issue exactly; I just needed to feel sophisticated and pretty instead of 13 and gawky. Not even thinking how this trendy French style might go over in our small farming community, I asked for and got this ultra-short haircut. I was quite pleased with the results, and I went to school thinking my junior high classmates would like my hair as much as I did. Boy, was I in for a rude awakening.

The kids were merciless in their ridicule of my lack-of-hair cut. Some just laughed at me, while others called me cruel names that still ring in my ears. I didn't go back to school for two weeks, waiting for my hair to grow out a little. Years later, it's still painful for me to think about.

When I think of the many hundreds of dollars I've spent on cuts, color, sprays, shampoos, de-frizzers, deep conditioners, herbal essence shampoos, BAD HAIR DAY baseball caps. . . . All for the sake of flat vs. fluffy.

Have I ever fretted so much about the unsaved people in China?

BAD-HAIR DAYS IN THE BIBLE

You think bad-hair days are just a media-driven concern of modern times? You'll find quite a few botched coifs in the Bible. Take Samson, for example. Here's a guy with great looks, incredible physical strength—a superstar athlete in his day. And his secret grooming tip? Don't cut the hair.

"No razor has ever come upon my head," he let slip one day, "for I have been a Nazirite to God from my mother's womb. If I am shaven, then my strength will leave me, and I shall become weak, and be like any other man" (Judges 16:17, *NKJV*). Smitten by Delilah, Samson revealed to her the secret of his great strength. And before Samson could say "Just a little off the ends," Delilah had his locks shorn and Samson was easily captured by the Philistines.

Later, when his hair grew back and he got his priorities in order, Samson brought down the house in his final performance.

*Hair today, gone tomorrow. "I will rather boast about
my weaknesses, that the power of Christ may dwell in me"
(2 Corinthians 12:9).*

On the other extreme, there's the prophet Elijah, who was
naturally bald. This man of God became upset when teens made
fun of his hairless head. The story is told in 2 Kings 2:23,24.
Elijah was on his way to Bethel when a large group of young men
from the city surrounded the prophet and began mocking his
bald head. Not appreciating their sense of humor, Elijah pro-
nounced a curse on them. And what a curse! Two female bears
lumbered out of the woods and made lunch of 42 of the youths.

Yes, hair has been a big problem since Eve left the Garden
without packing a hairbrush. Maybe that's why God numbered
our hairs—so we wouldn't have to worry about them.

THE ULTIMATE STYLIST

You probably don't have a team of hairstylists who make you look picture-perfect every morning, and that's OK. After all, you were fashioned by the ultimate stylist. God created you to be an imperfect person who finds perfection in Him. It all goes back to the days of Eden.

When God created man and woman, He saw that we were good. Not perfect, but good:

> And God saw all that He had made, and behold, it was very good (Genesis 1:31).

Phew! The pressure's off. We're not supposed to be perfect like the models we see on TV. This is a big comfort to me, especially when I catch a glance of my backside in one of those rearview dressing-room mirrors. Why should I expect more of myself than God does? My body will always have a few lumps of imperfection, just like my gravy. But that's OK. Recognizing that I fail to measure up to the world's impossible standards of physical beauty helps me to focus on where my adequacy really comes from:

> Not that we are adequate in ourselves to consider anything as coming from ourselves, but our adequacy is from God (2 Corinthians 3:5).

Paul goes on to remind us in his letter to the Corinthians that God shines in our hearts and that we carry this treasure "in earthen vessels, that the surpassing greatness of the power may be of God and not from ourselves" (2 Corinthians 4:7). Will someone please forward this letter to the editors of *Cosmopolitan*, *Elle* and those other magazines with seductive supermodels displayed next to the Junior Mints at my supermarket checkout stand!

I used to read fashion magazines, hoping to feel better about myself, only to end up getting more depressed. The self-help articles told me that my adequacy comes from perfectly plucked eyebrows and jiggle-free thighs and that my worth as a person was measured by the activity in my social life. Considering that my big Saturday-night date was usually with a laundry machine, I often felt like a Leah in a world of Rachels.

The Bible tells me otherwise. My worth comes from being a child of God, and He has given me His Spirit to help me measure up to His specifications, bad-hair days or not.

UNREAL STANDARDS

True, the impossibly perfect images we see on TV and in magazines are hard to ignore. Even I forget that advertising is not reality, and I'm one of those who help create the illusion!

Take for instance those commercials featuring models with bare shoulders and long, silky, shimmering hair. Believe me, it takes more than the shampoo being advertised to create hair that looks like that. To create the illusion of devastatingly perfect hair requires lots of time and money.

First, there's the search for the ideal hair model. The condition of her hair is as vital as her smile, so it's not unusual to search internationally to find one model with fabulous hair. Once the model is found, we begin filming the commercial—a process that takes a lot longer than 30 seconds. The first day of filming is stuff you never see. This is a day set aside for "hair exploration," a very expensive version of what teen girls do at a slumber party. The director and advertising agency hover about the chosen model, running through different set-ups, styles, configurations and scenarios to learn just what will make her hair look its absolute best. Are bright lights or dim lights called for? Does her hair look better in the morning or afternoon? How many times can she run her fingers through her hair before it needs to be restyled?

There's usually a SWAT team of hair specialists standing by to assist the model during filming, including a stylist and haircutter and someone who can fix frizzies on the spot. And you wonder why you can't re-create her hair in five quick minutes at home! No wonder the apostle Paul had his head shaved after his conversion. That way he wouldn't have to deal with this nonsense.

THE SECRET TO BETTER-LOOKING THIGHS

*We look not at the things which are seen, but at the things
which are not seen; for the things which are seen are temporal,
but the things which are not seen are eternal.*

2 CORINTHIANS 4:18

Even your favorite foods get a beauty treatment under the TV spotlight. Fried chicken that looks too good to eat probably is. Oversized plastic raisins are created to make the wrinkles prettier. Burgers get a face-lift, too. Special food stylists use tweezers to perfectly place sesame seeds on the buns, and tiny scissors to carefully cut up lettuce into perfect shreds. Brown edges are snipped off the side order of fries, too.

If you're wondering why so much attention is paid to such small details, it's because people like me are breathing down the stylist's neck. Commercials are little more than beauty contests for food, and you've got to treat that burger with as much care as you would Miss New Jersey before she walks down the aisle.

Thank God that His standard of beauty is not pickle deep. In fact, it has nothing to do with outward appearances at all.

Unseen Beauty

And let not your adornment be merely external—
braiding the hair, and wearing gold jewelry, or putting
on dresses; but let it be the hidden person of the heart,
with the imperishable quality of a gentle and quiet spirit,
which is precious in the sight of God.

1 PETER 3:3,4

According to God's standards, beauty cannot be achieved with wrinkle creams or pierced navels, so don't expect your mansion in heaven to have a full-length mirror. Proverbs 31:30 reminds us that, after all, a women's physical beauty is fleeting, which is why teens laugh at their parents' senior high school pictures.

Standards of physical beauty change over time and vary from one culture to the next. On our mission trip to China, I visited remote places where there were no McDonald's or ash blondes. As for the people living there, they had seen a Caucasian only on rare occasions. The native Chinese had very rich, black hair, petite features, smallish eyes and dark, weathered skin—all of which was beautiful by their standards. So when we showed up with our fair skin, peroxide roots and spicy deodorants, they stared at us like we were the newest attraction at the Beijing Zoo. And they didn't think we were particularly attractive, either. As a matter of fact, they laughed at our big noses, extra large feet and pale skin. Obviously, their standards of beauty were different from ours, but hopefully the impression we made as representatives of Christ was bigger than our noses.

DAVID, AN IMPERFECT ROLE MODEL

*"Do not look at his appearance or at the height of his
stature, because I have rejected him; for God sees not as man
sees, for man looks at the outward appearance, but the
LORD looks at the heart."*

1 SAMUEL 16:7

God made even the best of us to be imperfect humans. King
David was as human as they come, and the Bible doesn't try to
hide it. David was a shepherd, a warrior and a king. He bravely
fought and killed Goliath and created beautiful music for Saul,
who was king before him. But David made mistakes, too, including adultery and murder-by-proxy. He had an affair with a married woman, Bathsheba, and to make matters worse, had her husband killed by sending him to the front line of a fierce battle.

David's family travails weren't the stuff of prime-time sitcoms,
either. His children caused him all kinds of pain and sorrow. One
child died as a baby. One son raped his daughter. Then another son
killed that one. David's home life wouldn't measure up to the
world's standards for a role model today. Instead, his woes would
be splashed all over tabloid magazines and talk shows. Still,
David's imperfections led him to a greater dependency on God—
and that is where true strength is found (see 2 Corinthians 12:9).

IMPERFECT ≠ REJECT

Although we are not perfect, we as God's children are far from
rejects, for "love covers a multitude of sins" (1 Peter 4:8). We're
all human, some more than others. I'm definitely on the "more
human" side. I make mistakes with people. I make mistakes at
work. I make mistakes in selecting hairstyles. I make mistakes

with spelling and grammar that my editor thankfully corrects. At least in advertising, I usually have the opportunity to re-edit and correct what's less than perfect.

One incident that sticks out in my mind has to do with a custard product I was working on. We hired a professional announcer to provide the voice-over for this commercial. This announcer was extremely talented and someone I had used successfully on many projects. Therefore, I didn't even have her do a quick read of the script before the actual recording session. Once in the recording booth, I realized I had made a mistake. My announcer couldn't pronounce the word "custard"! (Hey, I can't pronounce "chrysanthemum.")

After 65 takes, our announcer could not say "custard" without the word sounding as if it were a tongue twister. It was funny and not funny at the same time; we needed to leave that recording session with something that worked. Our solution was to do some high-tech re-editing. We had the announcer substitute the word "mustard," which she had no problem saying. We later edited out the "m" sound and replaced it with a "k" sound. Editing can cover a multitude of "Schwinns."

Of course, it doesn't happen that way in real life. We can't edit out our mistakes and usually the mistakes we want to edit out are a lot worse than mispronouncing a word. Several years ago, my oldest sister enjoyed a reunion with a couple of friends from college. As they caught up on their lives since school, the conversation naturally wandered to the topic of careers and the stresses of the workplace. One of her friends was a printer and worked for a big printing press. He said, "If I make a mistake at work, I could cost my company thousands of dollars!" Being a pharmacist, my sister worked with drugs that could save people—or kill them. She quickly replied, "Well, if I make a mistake at work, I could cost someone their life!" The remaining friend then added, "I work at a nuclear power plant, and if I make a mistake at work, we can all go."

When you do make a mistake, it's a comfort to know that you are not a mistake yourself. God can edit out the mistakes of your past, even if you can't. You may not have blown up a nuclear power plant, but perhaps you made a mistake in your past that was harmful to you or someone close to you. Just remember that during life's "oops!" you *can* draw closer to God. David did, Samson did and you can, too.

SO FEAR GOD, NOT CELLULITE

A coworker was working on an ad for undergarments for plus-sized women. The agency decided to use a famous "real size" model. In other words, she wasn't Twiggy, but was more voluptuous and curvier. My friend was very impressed with this model's attitude. Far from fretting over her weight, she allowed her size to actually enhance her beauty!

Funny thing is, as the photographs were being prepared for the ad layout, several people commented that the plus-sized model didn't look "plus" at all. The self-image she projected was so positive that you looked past her figure's shortcomings. They were actually considering airbrushing weight *onto* her to make her look larger! Imagine that. Now imagine your self-image being that healthy. It can be when you find your identity in Christ.

No one is as perfect as the commercial characters we see on television—not even the actors who play them! But my flaws and imperfections haven't dissuaded God from loving me, nor have they stopped me from becoming a youth leader, a friend and a writer. Actually, in many ways my shortcomings have probably helped. Bad hair has helped me to empathize with teens and how they feel in their awkward years. Chubby thighs help to remind me that real beauty comes from within. The mistakes I've made help me to forgive others when they make them, including the beauticians with whom I've shared so many misadventures.

My imperfections have led me to depend on God and place my trust solely in Him. I know that my worth comes from my life with Him, not from anything I can do or achieve myself. Paul had a thorn in his side. I have toxic orange hair. Whatever it takes to perfect my relationship with Christ.

FASHION TIPS THAT NEVER GO OUT OF STYLE

Still striving for perfection? Don't look for advice in magazines. Just remember these healthy hints on relationships and fashion from the Good Book:

PERFECT FRAGRANCE

> For we are a fragrance of Christ to God among those who are being saved and among those who are perishing (2 Corinthians 2:15).

PERFECT WARDROBE

> Put on the full armor of God, that you may be able to stand firm against the schemes of the devil (Ephesians 6:11).

PERFECT BODY

> I shall not be put to shame in anything, but that with all boldness, Christ shall even now, as always, be exalted in my body (Philippians 1:20).

PERFECT LOVE

There is no fear in love; but perfect love casts out fear, because fear involves punishment, and the one who fears is not perfected in love. We love, because He first loved us (1 John 4:18,19).

PERFECT RELATIONSHIP

"I in them, and You in Me; that they may be made perfect in one, and that the world may know that You have sent Me, and have loved them as You have loved Me" (John 17:23, *NKJV*).

PERFECT WAY TO HAVE IT ALL

And let endurance have its perfect result, that you may be perfect and complete, lacking in nothing (James 1:4).

THE PERFECT MAKEOVER

But we all, with unveiled face, beholding as in a mirror the glory of the Lord, are being transformed into the same image from glory to glory, just as by the Spirit of the Lord (2 Corinthians 3:18, *NKJV*).

Chapter 14

Plugging into God

In the summer of 1997, *The Truman Show* opened in movie theaters and became an instant hit with critics and audiences alike. Comedian Jim Carrey toned down his trademark zaniness to convincingly portray Truman Burbank, the unwitting star of the world's most popular TV show. Christof, the producer of the show, had created a massive artificial environment complete with hundreds of actors and extras who populated the mythical town in which Truman was born and raised. Without his knowledge, 5,000 hidden cameras recorded Truman's every move, broadcasting his life to a captivated worldwide audience 24 hours a day—even while he was sleeping!

If someone taped your life, would it be worth watching? I've asked myself that question many times, especially thinking back on how much of it I spent watching reruns of "The Brady Bunch" and "Gilligan's Island." I know every "Brady" episode by heart, including my all-time favorite when Marcia meets Davey Jones. Growing up, I watched a lot of TV because there wasn't much else to do in the small Michigan farm town where we lived. The place was boring. There were no movie theaters (and still aren't) and no McDonald's. Just one stoplight and a lot of fruit trees.

When we weren't watching one of the three TV channels (four if the wind was right), my friends and I would get into mis-

chief, indulging in such typical teen high jinks as launching fire
bombs into outhouses or decorating neighbors' lawns with toilet paper. Or we would just sit in the parking lot of the town's
only grocery store and watch cars go by. While we thought we
were doing a lot of nothing, we were actually developing some of
the closest friendships of our lives.

As we sat in the grocer's parking lot, we would dream about
what our lives would be like if we lived in Chicago. Surely if we
lived in a big city, our lives wouldn't be boring. Chicago was only
about a hundred miles away and we went there every year for our
school field trip. The big city had movie theaters, museums,
McDonald's *and* Burger King and definitely more exciting
things to do than watch traffic. Chicago seemed to be a place
where boredom didn't and couldn't exist.

Little did I know that someday I would be a youth leader in
Chicago, where I would hear teens tell me the very same thing:
"Our lives are so *boring*! If only we didn't live in *Chicago*, things
would be different." These teens had access to activities I only
dreamed of when I was their age, so I was shocked to hear they
suffered from the same boredom I had.

But it didn't stop there. When in London, I was surprised to
find that teens there were plagued with boredom, too. One of
the first things I heard out of the mouth of a London teen was
"My life is boring; if only I lived in America, things would be different!" Hearing the familiar refrain in a thick cockney accent
didn't make it sound any better. Is there *anyplace* where boredom
isn't a problem?

It's easy to blame our boredom on our zip codes or lacklus-
ter network programming. But small towns don't give us small
dreams any more than television turns us into couch potatoes.
We are only as exciting as what we are plugged into, and for too
many of us, that means "Laverne and Shirley" reruns.

BOREDOM IN BETHLEHEM?

The soul of a lazy man desires, and has nothing; but the soul
of the diligent shall be made rich.

PROVERBS 13:4, *NKJV*

Have you ever read a Bible story about a prophet being bored or a disciple complaining he had nothing to do? They were too busy healing the sick, battling giants, moonlighting as spies and being all that God wanted them to be, doing all that He wanted them to do.

For 125 years, Noah was too busy building a boat in his backyard to be bored. He didn't have the friendly help of a hardware store, either. And when he finished that, he had to go out and gather two of every animal. Just where do you start looking for a pair of rhinos?

Think of Peter. There's a fisherman who wanted to catch more than a big tuna. Peter wasn't satisfied with sitting on the sidelines of life, especially with Jesus around. Take the time when Jesus walked on water. Peter was with the other disciples in a boat when it happened. But Peter couldn't just sit there; he had to get out and try to walk on water, too. So what if he got his feet a little wet? Now that was an experience Peter would never forget. But for the other disciples, it was just another boat ride. In an ark, in a boat or in a nutshell, if you're doing something for God, you won't have time to be bored.

PLUGGING INTO POWER

I am the vine, you are the branches; he who abides in Me, and I in
him, he bears much fruit; for apart from Me you can do nothing.

JOHN 15:5

Somewhere along the line, the world and even people in the Church got the misconception that this Christian stuff is boring. Yeah, right. Nothing adds more excitement to life than living for Christ. God made you. He knows your talents and your dreams. If you stay connected to Him, you can be all He wants you to be. It's really a no-brainer. Still, we are tempted every day to plug into anything *but* God. Maybe if God equipped each of us with a two-prong plug, the spiritual dynamics would be easier to understand.

Just suppose for a moment that on the sixth day, right after putting the final touches on the zebra and kangaroo, God didn't make humans in His own image, but instead made us to look like TVs. We would each be a top-of-the-line model, with high-definition picture, a plug and, of course, a lifetime warranty. Now since we'd have all the features of a television, we could tune into a wide variety of programming, from local news to game shows to "The Flintstones" reruns. With nearly infinite possibilities, we could tune into whatever we desired or imagined—under one condition: we stay plugged in. Because if we weren't plugged in, we couldn't do squat. All we would be good for is collecting dust.

But we don't have plugs, just overactive imaginations. What's important to remember is that when you're plugged into God, an amazing array of possibilities opens up to you.

Take, for instance, how I got my job in advertising. All my life, all I ever dreamed of doing was working in advertising. Perhaps you dreamed of meeting the president of the United States; I dreamed of meeting the Ty-D-Bol man. This dream helped to sidetrack my relationship with the Lord, but once I made God's will for my life *my* priority, God opened the door for me to write. I left my small town and moved to Chicago, where I became a copywriter for a big advertising agency. Once there, the

Lord gave me the strength to get through each day and prosper. But as fun as advertising can be, it can't compete with the joy I receive from tuning into ministry.

TUNING INTO A MINISTRY

If you really want to get a charge out of life, why not tune into a ministry? You'll be pleasantly surprised when you find that you get as much out of it as you put into it. Getting involved in a ministry for God doesn't necessarily mean moving to a jungle in Timbuktu, either. There are plenty of ministries right in your own backyard in need of the special components God gave you.

I'm one of those insane individuals who willingly got involved with youth ministry. As a result, I might occasionally suffer from sleep deprivation or Doritos breath, but boredom? Never! My work with this ministry started when I ended up in jail on my birthday. I was attending a church that had established a ministry at Chicago's Cook County Jail. Volunteers in this ministry tutored the inmates in academic studies as well as the Bible. I had just moved to Chicago and didn't want to spend my birthday alone, so I thought, *Hey, why not go to jail?*

Coming from a small rural town, I had no clue what I was in for. I expected Chicago's Cook County Jail to be like the one in Andy Griffith's Mayberry, with a scrawny little guard, a whistling sheriff and a friendly town drunk. In fact, Cook County was temporary home to hundreds of young men incarcerated for various crimes like gang shootings, drug dealing, armed robbery—all kinds of ways that idle minds can become the devil's workplace. This ministry was wonderful because Christ was the very thing these guys needed to get their lives back on track. Many we ministered to made a serious decision for Christ. Still, I got a pit in my stomach every time I went.

Seeing these young people in jail made me realize that teens needed to be reached *before* they wound up behind bars.

After a few years of jail ministry, God opened the door for me to volunteer with the youth ministry at my church. It was the perfect outlet for me to use my God-given creativity to help young people detour life's trouble zones.

EXTENSION CORDS FOR CHRIST

"Let your light shine before men."
MATTHEW 5:16

You don't have to be in a ministry to have a ministry. You can be an extension cord for Jesus Christ simply by extending to others the love He freely shares with you. You can do this by sending a note, saying a prayer, making an unsolicited phone call or by going out for coffee with someone who needs encouragement. Hebrews 3:12,13 tells us, "Take care, brethren, lest there should be in any one of you an evil, unbelieving heart, in falling away from the living God. But encourage one another day after day, as long as it is still called 'Today,' lest any one of you be hardened by the deceitfulness of sin."

NEVER A RERUN

Life is either a daring adventure or nothing.
HELEN KELLER

If your life is beginning to resemble reruns of a syndicated sit-com, maybe it's time to try something new for God. Like climbing a 1,300-step monument in the middle of nowhere. That's what I did with a Bulgarian youth group in a small provincial town called Wymen. We had been teaching these teens that their youth group was only as exciting as they made it, so it was their mission to find something to do together that would be very memorable.

Now, in this little Bulgarian town of Wymen there wasn't much of anything to do. No shopping, no malls, no fast food. Not even a grocery store parking lot where you could hang out and watch cars go by. There was, however, an interesting landmark at the edge of town: a monument commemorating the 1,300-year history of Bulgaria. This massive concrete structure depicted your typical monument stuff like horses and bigger-than-life men preparing for battle and was visible from miles away. But to get to it, you had to climb 1,300 steps with no air-conditioning in the blistering summer sun. Nevertheless, I encouraged the youth group to climb the monument just to do something different, because if you want to have a memorable life, you have to do memorable things. For me, it is still a vivid memory. But for these Bulgarian teens? Come to find out, every time someone new came to town, that is what they would want to do. Still, climbing those 1,300 steps together is something that group—and their feet—will never forget.

No batteries required—the power of God keeps going and going and going. But if you plug into other outlets for your happiness, like batteries they will soon wear out and need to be replaced.

Youth groups are great places for young people to combat boredom. Where else can a young person make the most of their gift for burping or celebrate Christmas in July? It was the pleasant memory of making pizza at a friend's youth group that played a part in my decision for Christ almost a decade later.

Whether it's volunteering to help with the youth at church, serving at the local rescue mission or just starting a regular morning devotional time, there are all kinds of new experiences waiting for you in the Lord's army. You can plug into more power before 6 A.M. than most people plug into their whole lives! So be all that you can be. Whatever new challenge you take on for God, you'll be glad you did.

READ YOUR INSTRUCTION MANUAL

And these words, which I am commanding
you today, shall be on your heart.

DEUTERONOMY 6:6

When you don't bother to read the instruction manual, you are the source of your own misery. Take me and my VCR. Yes, the clock is blinking at 12 A.M., and no, I do not know how to fix it. I can watch a video when I want, but I can't tape "Scooby-Doo" or make sense of half the buttons on my remote.

It's not that my VCR is any harder to figure out than the next guy's. I'm just too stubborn to read my instruction manual. Strangely enough, I am well aware that if I would only take the time to read it, I would likely get as much enjoyment out of my VCR as the manufacturer intended.

Well, the same holds true with the instruction manual for life itself. I'm not talking about *The Seven Habits of Highly Effective People* or *All I Really Need to Know I Learned in Kindergarten*, but the biggest best-seller ever written. God Himself provided us with the ultimate guide to life, the Bible, and who better to write it than the Creator of life, the universe and everything? Sure, we can set it on our shelves and ignore it, but life would be a whole lot more enjoyable if we read it. Here are a few highlights:

TROUBLESHOOTING GUIDE

SOCKET TO YOU

Do not be arrogant toward the branches; but if you are arrogant, remember that it is not you who supports the root, but the root supports you (Romans 11:18).

USE IT OR LOSE IT

"For everyone to whom much is given, from him much will be required" (Luke 12:48, *NKJV*).

A LITTLE POWER GOES A LONG WAY

"For truly I say to you, if you have faith as a mustard seed, you shall say to this mountain, 'Move from here to there,' and it shall move; and nothing shall be impossible to you" (Matthew 17:20).

DISCONNECTED?

For I am convinced that neither death, nor life, nor angels, nor principalities, nor things present, nor things to come, nor powers, nor height, nor depth, nor any other created thing, shall be able to separate us from the love of God, which is in Christ Jesus our Lord (Romans 8:38,39).

EXPERIENCING TECHNICAL DIFFICULTIES?

[Cast] all your anxiety upon Him, because He cares for you (1 Peter 5:7).

NEED EXTRA VOLTAGE?

I thank Christ Jesus our Lord, who has strengthened me, because He considered me faithful, putting me into service (1 Timothy 1:12).

BLOWN A FUSE?

Be angry, and yet do not sin; do not let the sun go down on your anger (Ephesians 4:26).

STILL TUNED OUT?

But as many as received Him, to them He gave the right to become children of God, even to those who believe in His name (John 1:12).

PROBLEMS? CALL ANY TIME, TOLL-FREE

"And call upon Me in the day of trouble; I shall rescue you, and you will honor Me" (Psalm 50:15).

HOLY GUACAMOLE

A high-school classmate has come a long way since our days of watching cars go by. Cindy became a Christian a few years after graduation. She went on to Bible school and ended up a missionary in Russia.

Cindy and her husband, Bill, were stationed in Cheryabinsk, about a thousand miles east of Moscow in the remote country-side known as Siberia. The stories Cindy and Bill share of their experiences in Russia redefine the expression "living by faith." The less they had materially, the more faith they developed in God. After a year in the mission field, they returned to the United States to visit family and gather more supplies.

Space was a precious commodity when traveling, as Cindy and Bill were allowed to carry only two suitcases apiece back into Russia and the suitcases could not weigh more than 40 pounds. Every item in their luggage had to be thought out carefully to make sure it was worth its size and weight. After much delibera-tion, Cindy decided to use a portion of her suitcase to pack two special items: peanut butter and guacamole mix.

Peanut butter is easy to understand, since it's an American favorite and quite expensive if you could even find it in Cheryabinsk. But the small foil pouches of guacamole mix? Cindy was determined to eat Mexican food in Russia. She knew she could find refried beans in Moscow—just a 36-hour train ride—and make tortillas from scratch. But find guacamole? Never. Still, Cindy was confident that she would get to dine on Mexican. If God could supply all her other needs, surely He could supply her with an avocado.

One day when Cindy was shopping in a small open market in Cheryabinsk, she noticed a lady trying to sell some dark-green shiny objects. This lady had no idea what they were; she didn't know if they were fruit, vegetable or even edible. Cindy couldn't believe her eyes. Those dark-green shiny things were avocados!

Cindy and Bill did more than eat guacamole and peanut but-ter in Russia. Along with leading others to Christ, they learned a new level of dependency on the Lord. If only Cindy and I had known in high school the adventures God had in store for us.

MUST-SEE TV

When it's all over, what will your life add up to? Will your life have been worth watching because of what you did for Christ? Or will you be just another pew potato? Plug into God today and discover the possibilities. It sure beats anything you can see on TV.

Chapter 15

And Now a Word from Our Sponsor

The tales I have shared with you from the strange and wonderful world of advertising are all true. My stories are often humorous, occasionally insightful or just plain weird. Hopefully, I have used these experiences to raise profound questions that go way beyond the mystery of why the Helping Hand has only four fingers. But a few of the memories from my career to date are painful and quite tragic, usually involving the lives of people I have known in advertising—extremely talented people who have devoted their lives to creating fun, memorable 30-second jingles and new ways to demonstrate toilet paper absorbency. People like Moe.

Moe was an immensely talented woman respected for her business sense and creativity. She started out as a copywriter and went on to become creative director, winning several awards along the way for commercials, campaigns, print ads and radio spots.

Moe had a good heart as well as good taste. She helped many to advance in their careers by pushing for promotions and opportunities they might not otherwise have had. Moe was always good for a dose of encouragement, and everyone who knew her agreed she was a breath of fresh air in a highly competitive business.

An abundance of energy was her trademark and at first, the hours Moe worked didn't seem all that unusual, because in advertising, everybody puts in a lot of hours. The satisfaction that comes with putting the final touches on a creative project is well worth the effort. But Moe found herself working more and more, soon becoming too busy even for her energy to maintain. Driven to excellence, Moe would put in the hours she believed necessary to get the job done.

One day, while getting ready for a major client presentation, Moe started complaining of a headache. She had experienced headaches before, but not like this one. The pain was so intense, she fell to her knees in the office lobby and grabbed her head as coworkers rushed to her side. Within moments, an ambulance arrived and Moe was taken to the hospital. Tests showed she had suffered an aneurysm in her brain. By the next morning she was dead.

This came as a horrific shock for everyone who knew her. Moe was only in her 40s with a husband and young daughter at home. Clients and friends flew in from all over the world for the wake. The vibrant woman with so much passion for life was gone. For a brief moment, art directors, writers and account executives all stepped back and examined their own lives: *What is the point of it all? Is my purpose in life merely to come up with new commercials?*

For a few months, the mood of the agency was changed by Moe's death. But little by little, employees became engulfed by their jobs once again, spending countless hours to find the perfect typeface or the ideal adjective to describe breakfast flakes.

TROPHY CASE

He who loves money will not be satisfied with money.
ECCLESIASTES 5:10

Another immense talent, Nick, was a big-time art director with a good eye, great taste and the guts to do breakthrough stuff. He worked hard and was highly respected for his sense of design. Nick won numerous awards and his name appeared in many award annuals. Eventually his name appeared on the door of his own agency.

But Nick's career got in the way of his life. As an executive, he spent more and more time at the office, and his marriage soon fell apart. He lost everything that mattered outside the office because of his devotion to work. Nick realized it wasn't worth it. So he took his name off the door, walked away from his corner office and became an art director again. An art director humble enough to work with someone like me.

To walk into Nick's office today, you would never know he had won so many awards. There isn't a sign of them anywhere. When I asked what happened to his awards, Nick chuckled. He said he put them where they rightly belonged, and he didn't mean a showcase, either. Nick took all his awards, his plaques, his honors and trophies and had one big bonfire. It was what Nick had to do to put his life back on track.

THE BIG PICTURE

If I could get a man to think for five minutes about his soul,
he is almost certain to be converted.
D. L. MOODY

Sometimes it takes a slap in the face to get back in touch with what life's all about. The slap could be a death, a major disappointment or just one costly mistake. A teen I knew made one bad decision that cost him part of his future. He became involved with a gang, which led to a fight and a 60-second act of stupidity that changed his life. This young man attacked a rival gang member with a baseball bat, and he spent several months in jail as a result. Sure, it gave him a lot of time to read his Bible, but it cost him his right to vote, a year of high school and the chance of getting any number of jobs. It took a felony charge to get this young man to refocus on God.

Sometimes I would get so caught up at work trying to find better ways to talk about two all-beef patties, special sauce, et al., that my focus on the big picture became blurred. It took a leave of absence and a stint doing mission work in Europe to help me get my 20-20 vision back. Climbing Bulgarian monuments and speaking in the British Bronx will always be cherished memories, but the one thing about this experience that did the most to open my eyes was something a coworker said when I returned to work in Chicago. Not knowing where to begin to explain all that God had taught me over the previous months, I let my coworker share with me her big news first. "You missed the best summer," she said. "We got the panty hose account!"

Is that what it's all about?

CONSUMERS OR CONSUMED?

You are worthy, O Lord, to receive glory and honor and power; for You created all things, and by Your will they exist and were created.
REVELATION 4:11, NKJV

Do you have any idea why cotton swabs were created? To look at them, you'd think they were made to be stuck in you ear. If you read the package, you'll find out differently. Now think, what is *your* purpose in life? When all is said and done, what will have consumed you?

Unlike those as-seen-on-TV products with 1,001 uses—"It slices, it dices, it sorts your mail"—God created people for one reason only: to worship Him. Abraham knew this better than anyone. He sacrificed his all to God and he was willing to sacrifice his only son, Isaac, at God's command. Now Abraham's descendants are as numerous as the stars in the skies and the grains of sand on the beaches (see Genesis 22:15-18).

Our world is filled with people who worship the Lord daily through their actions. For instance, anyone who prayed for you today. Anyone who put another's needs before their own. Anyone who showed patience to the person ahead of them writing a check in the "cash only" lane. Such people don't just *need* God; they *crave* God and their actions show it.

So during your brief stay on this planet, between commercial breaks turn off your TV and take time to realize the point of it all. You're not here just to be a consumer of spicy aftershave and candies with caramel nougat centers. And your biggest concern shouldn't be bigger, bouncier hair. After all, the one thing that will bring you joy for a lifetime and beyond is something you *want* as much as you *need*. Don't wait until a catastrophe occurs to allow yourself to be consumed by God. Live according to the purpose for which you were created. And remember:

Praise the LORD!
Praise God in His sanctuary;
Praise Him in His mighty expanse.
Praise Him for His mighty deeds;
Praise Him according to His excellent greatness.
Praise Him with trumpet sound;
Praise Him with harp and lyre.
Praise Him with timbrel and dancing;
Praise Him with stringed instruments and pipe.
Praise Him with loud cymbals;
Praise Him with resounding cymbals.

Let everything that has breath praise the LORD.
Praise the LORD!
(Psalm 150).

Let that be one jingle you never get out of your head.

BONUS CHAPTER!

There's More to Life than Snap! Crackle! Pop!

So how does a nice Christian girl end up in advertising? Would you believe by building a gigantic polyester Buddha? Though many credit my foot-in-the-door to this foam rubber-filled creation, I know it was God who orchestrated my steps. Let me start at the beginning.

While you watched television programs, I watched the commercials. While you read newspapers and magazine articles, I read the advertisements. While you whistled the latest pop tunes, I sang jingles about toilet paper.

All I ever wanted to do was advertising. More than anything else, I wanted to create those 30-second blurbs about boil-in-the-bag cuisine and fresh lemon-scent cleaners. More than I wanted to walk on the moon. More than I wanted to become Miss America. And definitely more than I wanted to live for God.

Even as a kid, every project I did in school would be about advertising. I wanted to know everything there was to know about the business from how blindfolded taste tests were conducted to where the Man from Glad came from and whether they really did put naked people in ice cubes.*

Somewhere between the birth of Snuggles the Bear and the death of disco, I decided to go to college—the first step toward getting to the big time, or at least somewhere with a movie theater. Of course, I selected a college the way every midwestern teen does: on the basis of their football team. Fortunately, after a year of being at the "wrong school," I had an academic advisor honest enough to tell me I should transfer. So I went on to a school where I could begin to fulfill my advertising dreams, Michigan State University.

Michigan State was literally a thousand times bigger than my hometown. There was a decent business department, a decent English department, but most importantly, decent dorm food. So it's not surprising that I loved college and all that went with it.

Now, if the old saying is true that "an education is the stuff that sticks in your brain after you forgot everything you learned," my most important lessons were learned in the dormitory, where I made lifelong friends and memories. Actually, I enjoyed learning and took classes that encouraged me to write and gave me a taste of the business. My time at Michigan State went quickly and I really didn't disappoint my parents all that much, except for the time I jumped out of an airplane and broke my back, but that's a different story.

God really wasn't a part of my life yet, probably because there weren't any commercials for Him during "General

---

* I've never found the rumors of subliminal advertising, like putting naked people in ice cubes to sell soft drinks, to be true. By the time you had pitched the idea of naked people in ice cubes, then put them into the ice cubes using state-of-the-art imaging, then the ad went through its usual countless changes and somehow managed to survive the many-tiered approval process, the naked people would end up a fully clothed, middle-income, midwestern American family floating in a soda.

Hospital" and "All My Children." But after roughly four years of all-nighters, midterms and #2 pencils, I was just about ready to graduate when the seeds of faith that had been planted in my life finally began to germinate. Aunts, uncles, Vacation Bible School teachers, youth pastor from a church I visited *only twice* 10 years earlier—the seeds they planted were being fertilized and cultivated by two honest-to-goodness Christians in my dorm. One of these women was the resident hall assistant whose name I can't remember. The other is still a close friend. These two women got to see the fruits of everyone else's labor.

Although I didn't recognize it then for what it was, inside me there was a place of emptiness, a gnawing hunger for something I had never before experienced. I was longing to know genuine joy—the kind of joy that didn't come from partying. The kind that would last longer than the thrill of creating my first commercial. The kind of joy that was evident in the lives of my resident hall assistant and my friend.

It was then I knew God was tired of me sitting on the fence, so I went to my room and started praying. God's presence was as real in that dorm room as the smell of microwave popcorn out in the hall. At that moment I handed my life, my dreams, everything short of my student loan debt over to Him. It was scary. It was real. It was the best decision I ever made.

Meanwhile, there's a detail I forgot to mention.

A detail roughly the size of a sumo wrestler on steroids.

During the summer preceding my senior year, I constructed a Buddha out of foam rubber and polyester. Don't ask me why. It wasn't so much a religious statement as it was an expression of small-town boredom. I had to have something to do while watching the grass grow. Actually, the motivation for this project was my oldest sister's summer mission trip to India; the Buddha was to be a surprise to welcome her home.

I had planned for the Buddha to be about the size of a back-rest pillow that I could use while studying on my bed. The tummy would be the gut of the backrest, the soft, pudgy legs the armrests. But being as apt in Buddha construction as I am in horseback riding (see chapter 10), my measurements were a bit off. Actually, a few dozen bits off. The stretchable polyester fabric kept expanding in size as I filled it. A backrest that was supposed to be the size of a pillow ended up being bigger than a king-size bed!

That summer I made countless trips to Kmart to fill my shopping cart with foam rubber. The sales clerks thought I was nuts, as did my mother. To this day I am amazed that she allowed me to make the monstrous thing in her living room. Her rationale was that it kept me out of trouble.

By the time the Buddha was done, it looked like an overgrown Cabbage Patch doll that had joined a weird cult. So when the time came for me to return to college, Buddha was going with me. Those were my mom's orders. The two-hour road trip to Michigan State was the stuff of "I Love Lucy" reruns: people honking and gawking at the near-bare bottom blocking the rear window of our tiny Toyota. One hefty leg was hanging out each back window. Miraculously, we made it to the campus without getting killed. As it turned out, the drive was the easy part. Getting the Buddha out of my mom's car and into my room was a procedure comparable to giving birth—backwards. And talk about a big surprise for my unsuspecting roommate!

Before long, Buddha became very popular. People I didn't even know would stop by my room to see the "big man on campus." It was fun. A few months later I threw a party in his honor—the university's first and last Buddha-fest. This is the party that almost got me thrown off campus, if not for the intervention of my resident hall assistant, who saved my neck and Buddha's behind.

And before I knew it, Jesus wasn't just the sponsor of a couple of major holidays, but a loving Savior whom I wanted to walk with and talk with every day of my life.

Words can't describe the impact of those last weeks at college. I felt more than the presence of God in my dorm room; I felt the presence of God in my life. For the first time, I wanted to know God's will for my life. He created me and He probably knew what was best for me. So, after graduation, I put my dreams of big-time advertising on hold and looked for a copywriting job at a smaller agency near my hometown.

Meanwhile, I had to figure out what to do with my roly-poly polyester pal. I thought it might be fun to write to several major advertising agencies asking them for their creative advice on what to do with a "two-ton Buddha." Surely, if they could offer solutions for everything from halitosis to hemorrhoids, they could help me with my weighty problem. So I wrote a fun letter that said nothing about my wanting a job in advertising, nothing about my fresh, hot diploma, nothing about my desire to become the next Darren Stevens. All the letter said was that my mother wanted the Buddha out of the house now.

I mailed the letter along with a picture of my foam rubber friend to the first five big ad agencies I could think of. All I was expecting in return was something funny to read while I ate my Corn Flakes.

However, the response I received wasn't from your average copywriter, but from the chief creative officer of what was then the biggest advertising agency in the whole, wide world! What I read still gives me goosebumps. I couldn't get past the first two lines:

Dear Ginger,
We'll adopt your Buddha under one condition, if you come to Chicago to write commercials for us.

I was floored! OK, I was anything *but* floored, as enough adrenaline was pumping through my veins to propel me to the moon. So, I ran circles around the front yard with my dog. The neighbors thought I was nuts. The people I called with the news thought I was as nuts. My mom thought it was terrific, because the overgrown Buddha would be out of her house once and for all.

Two weeks later, I was writing jingles for Rice Krispies in downtown Chicago.

You must understand, jobs in advertising don't come around like this any more than they come like this in other fields. People pound the pavement for months, toting elaborate portfolios and hoping just to get their foot in the door. All I did was live by Psalm 37:4,5: "Delight yourself in the LORD; and He will give you the desires of your heart. Commit your way to the LORD, trust also in Him, and He will do it."

Though many people say Buddha got me the job, I am certain this was the work of almighty God. Not until I put Christ at the heart of my life did He give me my heart's desire. If I hadn't, I would still be leaning against that foam rubber tummy in my mom's living room with fading dreams of Energizer bunnies and scrubbing bubbles.

But that was back in 1983. Since then, much has happened.

First off, Buddha bit the dust. He was peacefully sitting in the corner of my modest Chicago apartment when I took a pair of sewing scissors to him, and before you could say Rice-A-Roni, my hulking creation was transformed into much-needed pillows. Though his belly is behind us, Buddha has become a polyester legend in the ad world. I have shared his story with many advertising interns as well as youth groups.

I stayed with that agency four years, writing commercials for breakfast cereals and pasteurized processed cheese. Wanting a taste of something new, I moved to another big agency where I worked on accounts for everything from supersized burgers to super-strength cleansers.

Since launching my career, I have learned a lot about advertising. Like the absurd amount of money one can make just for coming up with a new way to talk about tuna. Or the equally absurd amount of money a company is willing to spend just to "goose" the bongos on a commercial's music track. So much time, so many dollars devoted to disposable messages for offers that end at midnight tonight.

Eventually, the fundamental absurdity of advertising started to get to me. I mean, I could only work so long promoting panty hose, knowing that I could be helping the homeless. I was bothered about the amount of energy I devoted to a floor wax instead of a Bible study. That's when I volunteered at Chicago's Cook County Jail to take part in a Bible study for inmates. From there I got involved with the youth group at my inner-city church.

By the summer of '96, I was ready for a change. A big one. I decided to take a leave of absence in order to work with teens in Europe. I took over a youth pastorship in London, then traveled throughout Bulgaria where I continued to speak to teens. Every day was a new adventure. I was meeting Christians whose faith was the same brand as mine, but whose realities were totally different. From Bulgaria to the British Bronx, I saw how Christianity was not just Sunday fluff, but a faith that was holding lives together.

After such an extraordinary experience, it was difficult to return to my job. I could no longer get excited about working on hosiery. That's when I knew my commercial break was over. Actually, the exact moment was when someone came into my office to tell me about the exciting new flavors of instant mashed potatoes. I knew then it was time to tell the world about something more important than Garlic Herb & Chive, that being the gospel of Jesus Christ.

With much prayer and good counsel, I quit my full-time job in advertising to spend more time working with my church youth group. People knew I was quitting to join the God Squad, and I got lots of support from everyone, including top agency management. No more worrying about the proliferation of cheap generic products; now I'd be living on them. Though I wouldn't be making lots of money, I would have what money can't buy: enriched faith and enough courage to be the next Wheaties champion.

Today I work in advertising part-time in addition to working with the youth group. I've taken the tools I learned in advertising and used them to communicate the Christian faith, hopefully to make young people want Christ instead of being told that they need Him.

As much as I love working with teens, I know the world of advertising is a mission field, too. It's a field filled with people not so different from you and your friends. They need God, too, and most are looking in the wrong places for happiness.

Pray for the artists, designers, writers and others responsible for those clever commercials you see during the Super Bowl. Pray that someday they, too, will realize that the most important thing to tell the world about is not new, nor can it be improved. It's something that will not last for just 30 seconds or even a lifetime, but for eternity.

And that's the life-changing power of Jesus Christ.